The Ripple Effect

Memoirs from the Inside

THOMAS FLEMING

Copyright © 2021 Thomas Fleming
All rights reserved
First Edition

Fulton Books, Inc.
Meadville, PA

Published by Fulton Books 2021

"Some of the names have been changed to protect the not-so innocent".

ISBN 978-1-63710-093-6 (paperback)
ISBN 978-1-63710-094-3 (digital)

Printed in the United States of America

For my mother, who never gave up on me. Mr. F, your bravery will never be forgotten. You taught me the meaning of empathy and forgiveness. That was my catalyst for change.

Contents

Prologue: I've Been Everywhere, Except the Electric
Chair, and I've Seen Everything but the Wind 7

Chapter 1: Can You Smell That smell? 9
    Falling Deeper 12
    Anchors Away 15
    Quick Fixes 18
    Out of Control 21
Chapter 2: Doing Hard Time 25
    Sorry, Cuz 28
    Building a Reputation 29
Chapter 3: Nothing Has Changed 33
    That All-So-Familiar Sound 38
    A Way Out 40
    Don't You Know Who I Am? 41
Chapter 4: What Have I Become? 44
    Into the Belly of the Beast 48
    An Eye for an Eye 52
    Beat Me Down Like a Rabid Dog 55
Chapter 5: Don't Forget to Smell the Roses 60
    Bare Bottom Blues 61
    What Is a Normal Day? 62
    A Real Friend 65
    Who Put Out a Hit on Me? 67
Chapter 6: Can I Get a Hug? 70
    There's a Barnyard in Hell with a Countryside View 72
    Roll Up! You're Going to General Population 76
    I Refuse to Die in Prison 79

Chapter 7: Forgiveness 82
    Respect/Disrespect...86
Chapter 8: New Beginnings 89
    She Believed in Me 92
    God Has a Plan for You 94
    I'm in 7 Habits 97
    No Peeing in the Bucket 102
Chapter 9: Do I Want to Go Where, Sir? 107
    Northbound and Down..112
    Bloom Where You Are Planted 116
    The Boys Are Back in Town...119
    The Garden of Trust 123
    I Pray Crow Is Okay 126
Chapter 10: Providing Catalyst for Change 128
    Speaks from the Heart 130
    What a View...133
Chapter 11: Silver Linings 137
    Rising above Your Circumstances 139
    I Am Grateful to You, Dr. Covey 141
    Encouragement from Wally 144
Chapter 12: Giving Back...147
    Those That Pave the Way 149
    Ripples That Hurt 153
    Inspiration from Larry Wayne.......................................154
    I Have What? Cancer!..155
    Silverlinology..156
    Teachers Need Praises and Raises Too 160
Chapter 13: Rippling Reflections 163

Epilogue..165

Prologue

I've Been Everywhere, Except the Electric Chair, and I've Seen Everything but the Wind

"Man up. Man up, boy! You have at least ten years to do in this hellhole." With that said, I slapped myself across the face. That was August 31, 1991.

For the next thirteen years, I would periodically ask myself, "How the hell did I get here?" I was residing in a seven-by-nine-foot segregation cell within the infamous South 40 at the Nebraska State Penitentiary.

Have you ever wondered what a segregation cell looks like? Or what it can do to a man's psyche? I firmly believe the next step down on the ladder is death itself. There is nothing lower than being in the bucket, or what some call the belly of the beast, a prison within the prison. But did I belong there? I can answer that. Yes!

1

Can You Smell That smell?

I was born in 1960 and was raised in a one-bedroom duplex in South Omaha. It was Mom, Dad, my two sisters, and my younger brother. My sisters shared one half of the basement, and my brother and I shared the other half. My grandparents lived in the other half of the duplex.

Dad worked nights driving a forklift for a big chain grocery store. He would be sleeping when I woke up in the morning to get ready for school, and he was already at work when I returned home. Growing up, I was closer to my mom than my dad.

One thing I will never forget that has permanently marred my senses is the smell of beer. At the age of six, I distinctly remember standing in the alley next to our house. From there, I could see the big steam stacks rising high into the sky. The stacks were about two blocks away, and when they were emitting steam, it meant that Falstaff Brewery was in full production. When the wind was just right, the steam would drift down to where I was standing. I could feel the mist on my face, and I could smell the beer. I got a kick out of sticking out my tongue and believing that I could taste the beer.

I had learned to steal at a young age by hanging around the older kids that lived down the street. I stole twenty dollars from my grandmother Kula's cupboard, and I took my kindergarten sweetheart to the zoo. When I returned home, Mom asked me where I had been. Of course I couldn't lie about it. She had caught me with a sackful of toys and candy. I did lie about where I had gotten the money from. I told her that I found the money outside the corner bar lying on the sidewalk. Mom was madder at me because she had thought that I had spent all the money. Twenty dollars was a lot of money back in 1967. I had not received a spanking from my mom before this. She broke a paddle over my rear end, which made her even madder. The only solace I had after that spanking was that I knew I had about half of the money on me. Even at that age, I had the criminal sophistication to have hidden it in my shoe.

My friend Mikey lived in a house on the next street. Our backyards connected, and his older brother Billy worked at the brewery. On Friday nights, Mikey and I would pull this little red wagon up the street and behind the brewery. Billy would hand us cases of beer, and we would load up the wagon. Then we would cover up the beer with a blanket and take it to Mikey's house. We would put the beer in the refrigerator that was in their basement. In the early seventies, I could be found over their house shooting pool and listening to Alice Cooper on vinyl.

My grandpa, Adolph Kula, had a hand in raising me. He taught me how to fish, throw a baseball, and to sharpen a blade on a lawn mower. He also taught me how to drink. He was a great man who could do no wrong in my eyes, but he was also an alcoholic. My uncle, Gary Kula, had a drinking problem too, but he was my hero. It seemed we did everything together when I was a teenager. He was divorced and frequented a lot of taverns. I had the privilege of learning how to drive a car by being the designated driver for him. This was way before designated drivers were popular. I spent a lot of time in the bars and taverns meeting a wide variety of people who had a lot in common. I didn't know it at the time, but most of them had the disease of alcoholism. By the time I was sixteen, I had a drinking problem.

One of my distinct memories as a youngster was always going next door to my grandparents' half of the duplex on Sundays. I would watch my grandparents entertain their friends, including the priest from our parish. They would play poker a couple of times a month and drink. I never saw my grandmother Kula partake in any drinking. She was a lovely lady and one of the best hostesses I ever did see. She made sure everyone had enough to eat and drink. I was always my grandma's little helper. I used to go get everyone at the table their drinks. I even learned how to make a highball. It is when you mix 7 Up with Seagram's Seven.

When Gramps or Uncle would need a beer, I would be the one that went to go get it. When I opened the can of Budweiser, I'd take a deep drink from the can. I would walk back to the table and hand it to them. They would hold it as if they were weighing it, knowing I had drained about a quarter of it. They would always smile at me and then give me a wink. To me, this was their approval. I felt that I was being included in the grown-up stuff. The only problem was, by the third round of drinks, I could be found sound asleep, passed out in the front room.

For some odd reason as a kid, I always had the notion that I was adopted. Dad used to use his fists and occasionally his boots to discipline me. I was very rebellious as a kid. I remember one time after drinking at the apartment of a friend's sister, I decided to run away. I made it to the interstate and flagged down a car. It was in the middle of winter, and there was two feet of snow on the ground. When the driver opened the passenger side of the car door and asked me to hop in, I saw something in his eyes that scared me. Looking back at it now, I believe that my guardian angel was watching over me. I took off, and I ran back home to my mother. I had always found safety in my mother's arms.

There were a few times in my life that I had the opportunity to stay at my grandma Fleming's little house. She was a beautiful woman with a big heart. When I was about eight years old, Grandma and Grandpa Fleming came by my parents' house. They were on their way to South Dakota. They were going to attend my great-grandmother's funeral. When my grandpa opened the gate, he forgot to close it. My dog and companion, Tippy, a wiener dog, escaped and ended up getting ran over by a car. I was devastated. I told my grandpa that I hoped he got hit by a car and died too. The next day, I was told that my grandparents were in a car accident. They were hit head-on by a drunk driver, and my grandfather was killed. I blamed myself for the accident. I told myself that it was my fault that he died. Grandma Fleming passed away around the age of ninety. She always told me that she was praying hard for me. That was her thing, praying hard for me.

I had a few jobs when I was a teenager. My first job was stocking shelves at the corner meat market. It was the neighborhood store, and everyone in the neighborhood shopped there. It didn't take me very long before I started stealing cigarettes from the supply room. I was fifteen years old, and I didn't like the job. Mom told me that since I was eating like a horse and I had shown that I could work, I needed to look for a job that would allow me to work after school. I started to go through the want ads, and I found an ad for a truck washer. I went down to the terminal truck wash in South Omaha. It was located right behind the stockyards, and I applied for the job. I had to have my mom sign some paper about a job permit because I was only fifteen, but the boss was impressed with my attitude. I got the job.

Can you imagine what a bull rack (cattle truck) smells like? I learned to like the smell, only because my boss used to tell me that it was the smell of money. It took me a while to figure out that he made all the money. I was the one doing all the dirty work. I did learn to change and repair truck tires; I was really good at it. I didn't like the sheep trucks that came in. They all had four decks in them. I liked to eat (I was what they call big-boned). I had a hard time learning to crawl in those little spaces between the decks. A lot of times, the sheep crap was deep. Despite the odor, I cleaned the heck out of those trucks. Once I gained the trust of the boss, he allowed me to open the truck wash on my own. I would wash trucks in the evenings and on the weekends. This gave me the opportunity to get in the storeroom and steal new car tires. I would take them to my friends and trade them for drugs. This went on until I was getting too high to show up for work. I quit before they found out I was robbing them blind.

Falling Deeper

It was a rainy night in 1977. After a night of partying, I was dropped off at my parents' house. There was a police car and a fire department vehicle parked in front of the house. I saw a few uniformed men standing by the front door. My uncle Frank, who was a fireman at the time, was standing near them. He was talking to my mother. My life was about to take a drastic turn.

I was told that my uncle Gary Kula, who was my friend, mentor, and the man I looked up to more than my own father, was dead. I learned that he was at some girl's apartment, supposedly drunk. They assumed that he had passed out while smoking a cigarette. The apartment went up in flames. Sadly, it was a closed-casket funeral. My childhood hero was gone.

At the ripe age of sixteen, my grandparents gifted me my uncle's car. It was a 1968 Chevy Impala. I dubbed it the Space Mobile. I was soon getting high in the car, smoking pot, drinking beer, and occasionally tripping on acid. Whatever I could get my hands on, I would use to get high. This was how I lived my life through high school—getting high and eventually selling booze and drugs out of the old Space Mobile.

Even in high school, I did a lot of stupid stuff. I was not your typical teenager. I committed crimes. I broke into the bowling alley that was connected to the high school and stole hundreds of dollars from a small safe. I was an attention seeker. The only people I attracted were broken people like me. I attracted the ones that never felt accepted and the low self-esteem variety. This led me to heavier drug use and crazier friends. I was voted most likely to end up in prison by my senior classmates. Of course, I couldn't let them down! They seemed to know me better than I knew myself.

One thing I will never forget is the time I tried to kill my dad. I came home drunk and high one night. My father started in on me about something. He raised his hand to hit me. I knew the familiar look in his eyes. I backed up to give myself some room. I pulled a buck knife from my side; I always carried one on me. I told him, "No more. You will never hit me again." This pissed him off, and he took a few steps toward me. I raised the knife and advanced on him. He knew I was out of control and stepped back.

My mother stepped in front of him and said in a surprisingly calm voice, "No, Thomas. I will not allow you to do this." I looked at my mom and then at the knife in my hand. I started to cry. I believe I cried for the simple fact that my mother had stepped in front of him. I couldn't hurt my mother. I told him that he would never again put his hands on me. I packed a bag and I moved out. I am proud of myself because I ended up graduating from Paul the VI High School in 1979.

Living in drug house as soon as I was out of high school was not a smart choice, but it was all I knew. I had a shot at a good job in 1979 with my friend's dad at the Asarco Smelting Plant. This was a plant that refined lead. I messed it up because of my drug use. I would get high on crystal meth then go to work where the temperature would be over a hundred degrees. I was not the sharpest tool on the wall, but I thought I knew it all. One week before I completed my probation period and was allowed to join the union, I was fired for missing too much work. I would rather get high.

I celebrated my firing by going to a big concert at the Iowa State Fair. This turned into a mess as soon as I got there. A bunch of us were camping at this old rock quarry. I had been drinking and tripping on some good acid, when I decided to run naked into a swimming hole. As soon as I ran into the water, I hit a submerged tree stump with my foot and broke my toe. The next day, I stayed so high to kill the pain that I don't remember much of the concert.

Most of my life after high school was a blur. It was one big drug scene with motorcycles, parties, bars with bands, and strip clubs. There were so many faces and a lot of meaningless relationships that all blended together. It didn't help that my cousin's band practiced in the basement of my house. So it was one continuous party every day, all day and night.

In my neighborhood there lived some bikers. One was a patch holder in the local motorcycle club. I found new role models for my life. One thing about the lifestyle of a biker is that they don't like drug users that are on the needle. I was a full-blown needle-using addict by the time I graduated high school. My dream of running with the pack was short-lived. This didn't stop me from riding motorcycles and hanging out with the hard-core patch holders at the strip clubs. I knew that because of my needle use, I would never be anything more than an associate.

Anchors Away

One night, I thought that I had killed a guy. A bunch of us were at a local biker bar over in Council Bluffs, Iowa. I hung around Council Buffs a lot. That's where Christy and a lot of my biker friends lived. My cousin's band had just finished playing, and another band was on the stage. Between their sets, the drummer and my bro Shorty were getting into a heated argument. Then the drummer asked me, "What are you looking at?"

I'm violent when I drink, so I told him that I was going to hit him. Then I hit him. This guy went down and hit his head on a bar table. His girlfriend screamed that he was not breathing and that I killed him. I was ushered out and banned from the bar. I was lucky the guy didn't die, but I didn't find out until a few days later. By then, I had already talked to a Navy recruiter.

I decided to enlist in the Navy. I was out of control. My friends thought that I was crazy. I was just an out-of-control drunken addict. It seems all my life I have been running away from one thing or another.

Running away to the Navy was a good idea at first but proved to be a drunken addict's nightmare. I was in the last week of boot camp and got a furlough for the weekend. This was a chance to let loose. Of course, I do not remember any of it. I came back to the base late. The next morning, I had final exams. Needless to say, I flunked and had to do the final phase of boot camp again. This put me a few weeks behind, but I still got to go to A-School in Meridian, Mississippi.

A-School was a drunken mess. I was able to go to the Enlisted Men's Club, but that was short-lived. I got banned for being drunk and disorderly. After A-School, I took a plane home, and the whole family was there to greet me. They were very proud that I was doing something with my life. I had ten days' leave before I had to catch a flight to meet the USS *Ranger*, an aircraft carrier. I stayed high on cocaine, and so I don't remember much.

As soon as the plane took off, I was drunk and high on the stash I had with me. It was a long flight from Omaha to Singapore, with a lot of stops in between. I do remember flying over Mount Fuji. It was a majestic sight, and one that is embedded into my memory. As soon as I touched down in Singapore, I checked in with the ship. Then I crawled into my bunk and slept for the next three days.

The *Ranger* set off for a 120-day trip at sea with no docking. For the July 4, 1982, I was in the Indian Ocean anchored right offshore from Sri Lanka. The highlight was getting drunk and lowering a bucket with holes in it down to the water in hopes to scoop up a big jellyfish.

One thing I always had was a good work ethic. My problem was the dope. I would always allow it to take over, and then I didn't care about anything anymore. On the ship, I rose to the top, like cream on top of the milk. Being a ship's serviceman, I had access to the ship's stores and all the store's cargo holds. As I rose to the top, I gained more access to better merchandise. This gave me more opportunities to steal and barter.

I had a buddy who worked in the mail room. He had access to good whiskey and bourbon. This was a blessing to me. I would trade watches, radios, food, and cold sodas (which were a rare commodity in the middle of the Indian Ocean) for bottles of Jim Beam and weed.

All the good things in my life that made me happy would eventually be thrown away. My Navy career was no exception. Back in our home port in Coronado Bay, California, I was on ship restriction for violating one of the ship's rules: I decided to sneak off the ship. The only way to get off the ship was for me to crawl down a conveyor belt. This belt was used to unload trash off the ship. I would walk up to the belt and act like I was throwing the trash away. Then I would dive down into the muck that led to the dock. This dock was huge enough to allow not only an aircraft carrier to dock there but also a couple of battleships.

One thing that I loved about being stationed around San Diego, California, in 1983 was that the party scene was huge. I had a shipmate who was from the Los Angeles area. Having a friend that knew the area gave me an opportunity to go to the US Festival in San Bernardino, California. This was filled with big name bands, and as usual, I don't remember much of any of it.

One particular night, I was coming back from a night at the strip club in downtown San Diego. Instead of coming back in the usual handcuffs under escort from the shore patrol, I managed to make it back on base undetected. I had to sneak back on the ship. This was not an easy thing. I would put the clothes I was wearing in a bag then don on a pair of overalls. To get back on the ship, I had to run up the conveyer belt. Once off the belt, I could maneuver my way through the hangar bay. That's where all the planes were stored. I then had options on which staircase I had to take to get to my sleeping quarters.

As soon as I hit the stairs to go down a deck, one of the officers saw me. The chase was on. I ran through a couple of opened hatches and right smack into a Philippine master chief. This particular one didn't like me. The feeling was mutual. I hit him with all I had. He went down hard. Then it turned into an episode of the *Keystone Kops*. The ship's police were chasing me, and the master chief was trying to keep up with them. I hid behind a hatch door as three of the ship's patrol ran by. I could hear the master chief getting nearer. When his hard sole shoes hit the deck, they made noise with every step. I timed it just right. I stepped out from behind the hatch and hit him hard. Before I was able to do any damage to him, the ship's patrol was on me. They tackled me with so much force that they dislocated my shoulder.

This led to a long stint in the ship's brig. After a few weeks in the brig, I was back on ship restriction until my court-martial. I had no plans to wait around for my court-martial. I took what money I had saved and snuck off the ship. I called home and lied to Mom about getting leave. I told her that I didn't have a lot of money. I asked for her to wire me some money so I could purchase a bus ticket to get back home. A few hours later, I received the money. I bought a ticket to Omaha. I also had a pocketful of good California weed. I knew this was enough to stay high all the way back to Omaha.

Quick Fixes

After I returned back home, I ran into my childhood sweetheart. She was married at the time to another childhood friend whom I didn't like. She said that she was not in love with him and she was going to divorce him. We made a pact: I go back to the Navy and get my discharge, and she gets a divorce.

I didn't understand how she wanted to be with me now. Just a few years prior, I asked her to marry me, and she had refused because I had drug problems. I thought, *Well, she needs me now.* The truth was, I believed it would be an easy way out for me. I have a habit of running from one problem right into the next.

I turned myself in at Offutt Air Force Base in Bellevue, Nebraska. I was taken back to the USS *Ranger* for court-martial. I was sentenced to a few months in the Thirty-Second St. Brigg in San Diego, California. I also received an OTH. This stands for an "Other than Honorable Discharge." *My Navy career ended just as it started—a mess.*

I tried to stay straight and be cool while living at Mom's house. It didn't take me long to get back in the mix. The old friends, booze, dope, and messed-up relationships. I went to Christie's apartment to see my son. I found him sitting on top of the roof, all alone. His mother was passed out in the front room on the couch. When I woke her, she mumbled something about having a hard night at work stripping and partying. I asked her how many times the kid had crawled out the living room window. Evidently, this wasn't the first time he had been found on the little roof outside of the second-story window!

She didn't want custody of the kid because he had become a burden. She wasn't able to party like she wanted to. I looked at her real closely and saw how the meth was eating at her teeth. This once beautiful woman now looked broken down. It didn't take me long to have her put me on the boy's birth certificate. I took full custody of him. Here I was, all messed up. I couldn't even take care of myself. Now I was going to try to raise a two-year-old kid. For some odd reason, I thought this was the thing that would help me get my life straightened out. I was living in a fantasy.

I found the fix for the problem I created. I had talked Juki into getting married. Her divorce was finally final. I could create the perfect family. Mine plus hers would equal ours. She had two kids, and I had one. We would eventually have a son and a daughter together.

When Juki and I first got married, I came home to our apartment and found her with her ex-husband. She took a few minutes to unlock the chain on the door. She stood there in the foyer as her ex-husband was sitting on a bed that was in the kid's room. I saw his wallet on the kitchen counter. I blew my top. He got around me and shot out of the apartment before I could lay my hands on him. I tossed his wallet to Juki and told her to get the hell out of my sight. I never trusted Juki again. I did take some time to think the incident through. I came to the conclusion that she did cheat on her then husband with me, so what would ever stop her from cheating on me? My trust factor went to zero. Right then and there, I vowed to myself that no matter how messed up I was, I would never get involved with a married woman.

All this forced me to work hard so I could support my family. I went to work at a truck tire service center. I worked about sixty hours a week to make enough money to pay the bills. It didn't take me long to let the stress get to me. The only way I knew how to deal with it all was to drink my blues away. It didn't take long for me to receive a drunken driving ticket.

I received a suspended sentence and had to take what they call outpatient treatment. I also had to go to three AA meetings a week. There was a meeting right up the street from the house. That was where I met Art. I called him Art the Fart. He was a real down-to-earth man. We became close friends. He was sober for a few years, and we had a lot in common. I stayed sober for almost two years. Art and I created a bond. We went fishing together and attended AA meetings. Juki and I created a close friendship with Art; his wife, Corky; and their daughter, Heather. They lived up the street from us, and we had a great friendship. Art used to keep his Harley in my garage. We would work on his bike on the weekends. It was a pleasure to assist Art with the rebuild of his Harley.

My marriage eventually went bad. In hindsight, it was doomed from the start. This marriage was built on necessity and desperation. The more I worked, the more she would bitch at me and the kids. Her relationship with my son, Joseph, who was her stepson, was getting real bad. All I heard every night when I got home was what Joe did this time. I saw how she was picking on the kid. I made the decision to take my son to my mother's house to live.

As the months passed by, the pressure of having four kids took its toll on Juki. I was tired of the fighting all the time. Every day I would hear how it was my fault that her life was messed up. I handled it the best way I knew how at that time. That was to go out and get drunk. I found peace in the company of other miserable people in the bars. It was my old stomping grounds. It wasn't long before I bought a nice seventies-style chopper. I went back to my old ways: motorcycles, booze, and drugs.

My marriage to Juki got really bad to the point of her filing for divorce. We tried to patch it up a few times, but my drug use was out of control, and in the end there was no trust on either side. I often wonder if there was any trust at all in the beginning. At this point, I had been conditioned to have serious trust issues when it came to women. Even when I was with my oldest son's mother, before she was pregnant with Joe, we were having an argument. I stopped by her house and found a strange car in the driveway. I was my usual drunk and high self and proceeded to beat the door down. Christie's new friend tried to play the new boyfriend hero, and I thumped him up pretty bad. Was I the jealous type? He left and we got back together for a few weeks before the big bar fight that had me choose a Navy career.

On one attempt to get back together with Juki for the sake of the kids, we moved into a different house. I wasn't working and she had a part-time job, so I decided to rob a few places to put food on the table (at least that's what I used for an excuse). I sold almost everything that I had, including my prize possession, the chopper. This was to feed my addiction, not my kids.

I had long forgotten about the AA meetings, but I did have a so-called friend that I met at those meetings. I used to be a chairperson for Thursday night meetings, and after the meeting, I would go to the bar across the street from the AA Club. At the bar, I would sign all the cards for the guys that were on probation. They would buy me drinks in exchange. What a good gig I had going on, I thought. When the probation officer would call me to verify if that guy was at the meeting, I would say that the attendance record was a thing of anonymity, but off the record, yes, so and so was there.

Out of Control

It was the fall of 1986. I was totally out of control. One Friday night, I was getting drunk and ran out of money, so I decided to get some drinking money. Down the street from the local biker bar was a 7-Eleven, and I knew that I could get some quick cash there.

I walked in. There were two registers going at the same time, which meant double the profit. I put my hand in my pocket and told the women behind the counter to empty the money into a bag. This was a Friday night, payday for the middle class. As soon as I got the money, I took off on foot. I hightailed it up the street and into the familiar back alleys of South Omaha. These were my old stomping grounds.

Three blocks away, I knew a chick that was staying at her dad's house. They had a big backyard which was surrounded by a tall slated fence. No one could see through the fence and into the yard from the alley. I had Karen put the leather jacket I was wearing in her room. The cops would be looking for a man in a leather jacket. As I sat on picnic table in the backyard, I counted out almost a thousand dollars. The whole time that I was counting out the money, the police cars were circling the block and up and down the alleys.

About two hours later, Karen and I were making crazy love (it seemed that me being an outlaw turned her on). I made my way back to the bar, and I walked in. One of my bros told me that the cops were in the bar looking for a big guy in a black leather biker jacket. I laughed and bought the bar a round of drinks. I found the dope man and scored some meth. I partied all night long. I blew through all the money, not once thinking about my kids, bills, or a job.

By the end of 1986, I was strung out and needed money. The wife was on my ass, and the holidays were about here. No presents for the kids. I ran into Terry, an old acquaintance from the rooms of AA. We hatched a plan to rob a few places so I could get the wife off my butt. Maybe even have a good Christmas for the kids.

What I think about now is how messed up my thinking was back then. Here I was, robbing places and people for money so I could give the kids a holiday. But as soon as I got a pocketful of money, I would go to the bar and play the big shot. Give everyone a drink on me! Where is the dope man?

We pulled up to a video rental store. Videos were popular back then. As soon as we walked through the door, Terry with a knife and me with an ax handle, I yelled, "This is a holdup. Get your asses on the floor!" The young girl who was working behind the register wet herself and couldn't get down. I yelled again and she complied. We commenced to take all the purses and emptied the register.

Then this little kid who was lying next to his mother said, "Hey, mister, you want my dollar too?"

I said to him, "No, kid. You keep that." It was like I was playing some kind of a hero.

That incident still haunts me to this day. I might have messed that kid's mind up. I mean, hell, here I was telling a young kid, about ten years old, to keep that dollar. And the whole time, his mother was lying next to him, shaking in a puddle of piss, scared to death! What kind of monster had I become? I wish I could talk to that kid today. I would explain to him why I did what I did. I would make amends with him.

The first stop we made after the robbery was to the new strip joint that opened up in South Omaha. It was on Twenty-Fourth and L Street. Once again, I thought I was King Shit with a bunch of money. I even had a few nice purses to give to the dancers along with big tips. It didn't take long before the money ran low and we went on to the next score.

THE RIPPLE EFFECT

I told Terry, "Let's make one quick score and then go to Las Vegas to start all over. The cops won't find us there." Once again, I was running away from all my demons. We walked into the Taco John's about three blocks from the strip club, and I ordered some food to go because I was hungry. I was not thinking about robbing it. One of my friends was arrested for holding up the same Taco John's, and I knew there was a camera hidden inside the mirror. As soon as I got the food and paid for it, Terry said, "This is a holdup!"

I was like, "Oh shit, here we go."

We pulled out of the Taco John's in Terry's Bronco and hit the highway. We were now on our way to Vegas. I passed out in the Bronco around Red Cloud, Nebraska. When I woke up, we were pulling into Omaha.

I said in a pissed off voice, "What the hell are you doing back in Omaha, Terry?"

He decided that he wanted to go back home because he was missing his wife. He thought he could work out whatever differences they had been arguing about. The only reason he went on a robbing spree with me was because he was mad at his wife.

I was sitting on the couch in the front room of Terry's house, watching myself on Crime Stoppers. I left Terry's house and went to find Juki and the kids. She was home but was hesitant on letting me through the door. After a few minutes of listening to her bitch, I pulled out some money. Juki shut her mouth up real fast and opened the door to let me in. She only wanted the money. She didn't care if I stayed or left. It was all about the money.

The first week of the New Year, I was sitting at home with the kids and Juki. I went to the kitchen and got a weird feeling that I was being watched. I thought I saw some movement in the alley behind the house. I went back into the front room, and I told Juki that I thought I saw someone move around by the tree in the backyard. It wasn't two minutes later. There was a knock on the front door. I knew that it wasn't good. I had locked the door that led to the front porch. Whoever was knocking had to pick the lock on the porch door to get on the porch to be able to knock on the front door. I had my youngest boy, Tommy, in my arms when I opened the door. A plainclothes cop had a gun pointed at me. He was telling me to put the boy down and step outside.

I stood there getting handcuffed, and all the kids were in the bay window waving at me. I just lowered my head. Then my youngest son, Tommy, came up to me. All he wanted to do was give his pops a hug. Juki held him close to me so he could wrap his little arms around me and tell me goodbye. I could only smell crap. The boy had on a shitty diaper. I thought, just like my luck, shitty.

I wasn't in jail but a few weeks, and here came the divorce papers. I found out Juki was already seeing another guy from the old rooms of AA. Come to find out, she had been stepping out on me for quite a while. In hindsight, the truth was that she had been sleeping around on me way before we were even married. What a fool I had been. But hell, I was an addict and a drunk. I tried to justify it in my mind by thinking that I didn't cheat on her until I found out she was cheating on me. Cheating is cheating!

2

Doing Hard Time

County jail was a trip. I had forged some good friendships while I was in there. One was with Jimmy T. Jimmy had a brother who would put weed inside the binding of a Bible. He would then have it mailed into the county jail. Everyone in that cellblock was getting Bibles. As soon as the guard would hand it to them at mail call, I would roll into their cell and confiscate it. Then I would take it back to our cell and pull the weed out of the binding. Once I would get the weed, I would then give the dude his Bible back. It was a good gig, and we stayed high for a long time.

Another old convict taught me how to cook pruno, prison beer. Some of the men in the jail called it hooch. It seemed there wasn't a day that went by that I wasn't stoned on weed or buzzed on hooch. It was something I used to escape reality with.

At night, I would think about Grandma Kula and how I had let her down. It was about a year earlier when I had received a phone call. She was in the hospital, in intensive care, and was on her deathbed. When I walked in the hospital room, I saw her lying there. She had all these tubes sticking out of her. I lost it! She woke up when I took ahold of her hand. She found enough strength to ask me to promise her that I would not end up like my uncle Gary or Grandpa Kula. They were both full-blown alcoholics. I gave her my word that I would not. She died a few days after that.

That is one promise that haunted me for years. Today I am proud to say that I know my grandmother is looking down upon me and smiling as I write this. Because not only have I been clean and sober for almost nine years, but I am also sharing the lessons of my life with others. We all have that ripple effect in our lives. Our actions can hurt or help people. Today I help people instead of hurt them.

In the spring of 1987, I was sentenced. The judge handed down a three- to seven-year sentence. This was to be served in the Nebraska Department of Corrections. As the prison van traveled down the highway, my only thought as we passed through the city of Omaha and on our way to Lincoln was that I wouldn't see my South Omaha for a long time. I didn't think about Juki or my kids. I didn't think about my family or friends either. I had become very self-absorbed.

I know most people have the same feeling when they hear the big steel door slam behind them when they enter the prison for the first time. I was no exception. It actually hurt my ears at first, but like everything else in the prison system, I would eventually block it out.

In the Diagnosis and Evaluation Center, known as D&E, I would not only learn the ways of the system but would also thrive in it. I and an old-timer, who taught me how to play pinochle, would walk around the yard. While we were getting our exercise, he would hip me to the ways of the prison hustle. I would soon learn it was not much different than the streets. The men in prison were cast out from society, the worst of the worst. Some were the dumbest of the dumb, and others were the lowest of the low. I found myself in the midst of killers, robbers (such as myself), burglars, forgers, arsonists, rapists, and the lowest of them all, the child molesters.

D&E was a fishbowl. Everyone went through D&E for evaluation. Even the parole violators had to go back through D&E. So I was schooled in the dos and don'ts of the prison system. Old Butch introduced me to the old convicts he knew. Since I was in for robbery, I fit in.

It wasn't long before we were taking everyone's money on the pinochle table and the poker table. I didn't want for nothing. I met the dope man, so all was good in my life. Here I was, making money, getting paid in commissary, and trading it for pot and speed. One other thing I found out was I could score a rig (syringe). This was heaven for a junkie. Prison may not be too bad, was what I thought.

THE RIPPLE EFFECT

I ended up being assigned to the Substance Abuse Unit at the Lincoln Correctional Center (LCC). For the first nine months, I was playing the recovery game. I would go to the classes during the day and get high at night. The prison hooch was excellent and was made in various ways. Each way would get the job done.

I knew how to get over and use my biggest asset—the ability to lie. I made it through the program and moved from the program housing unit. I was placed in housing unit B, which was known for being party central. What a difference there was. There was nothing but weed, meth, hooch, and the occasional angel dust. I was in a junkie's paradise.

I found a job washing pots and pans in the prison kitchen. This was an opportunity for me to use my hustling skills. I would steal whole pork roasts and whatever else I could get my hands on. I would trade these things for drugs, prison commissary, and to pay off the occasional poker debt when my luck would run bad. Imagine me having bad luck. Here I was in prison talking about bad luck.

One thing I did learn was not to get ahead of myself. I now know that a man creates his own luck. It's called cause and effect. If I make positive choices in life, then most of the time I will have positive results. I wish I knew this at a younger age, but then I wouldn't be the man I am today. I wouldn't change too much about my life except the fact that I hurt people. Everything that I did is who I am, right or wrong. These are the things that make up the fabric of my life.

I will never forget the day I was sitting in the dayroom at LCC. I picked up a newspaper that was lying there. It was about two weeks old. As I turned to the obits, I saw my grandfather's name. My world stopped. I had to find out that he passed away from an old newspaper. My own family didn't even tell me. I felt that they didn't want me to show up to the funeral in chains. They thought I was an embarrassment to the family. Wasn't I? For them not to tell me and me finding out from an old newspaper reassured me that I was truly the black sheep of the family.

I found comfort in getting high. That's how I coped with everything: get high and forget about it. The guy that lived in the next cell from me came back from a visit. He walked over to my cell and asked me if I wanted to try some wet, which is a potent form of formaldehyde used to get high. I never tried it, so I said, "Hell yeah!"

One thing about embalming fluid, it's way better than an acid trip, or so I thought. When I dipped a stick of weed in it, lit it, and smoked it, my world changed. I felt nothing. When I walked around after getting high on it, it was as if the pavement was rolling. I had a hard time walking.

Big Red stopped by the cell to drop off some Dexies. He was getting prescription Dexedrines, and to me, it was the purist form of speed a guy could get, in or out of prison. For the rest of my time at LCC, I would get higher than a kite. I would forget about the world I used to know and all the people in it.

Sorry, Cuz

Back to the present day for a minute. I may jump back and forth for a spell. My uncle Frank, the patriarch of the family, came to visit me along with my uncle Carl yesterday. They proceeded to tell me that my cousin Dean still thinks I hate him. You see, back in 1987, when I was medicating myself in prison, I wrote my cousin Dean. I tried to put a guilt trip on him for money. I needed to continue to feed my addiction.

Dean had a band that used to practice in the basement of the house I stayed at. It was a party house that I lived in, and I didn't even know who the landlord was. It was a house that one of my bros, Melvin, and his family lived in. When they moved out, I moved in. The landlord never did show up, so it ended up being an all-day party, every day!

Dean ended up quitting the band and the party life. He became a highly respected fireman. I was proud of him for getting out of that lifestyle. I did not have the testicular fortitude to do something positive with my life at that time.

As I sat in prison, I felt that Dean was out there doing well. With him having his life together, I thought I could play on his emotions and get some money out of him. I was a terrible person with no regard for anyone. Let's be honest. Here I was, a junkie making junkie moves.

For the past thirty years, my cousin Dean thought I hated him for not helping me. Talk about the ripple effect! There it was, plain as day. What a terrible, selfish person I used to be. The ripple effect is what life is all about for me today. It is what changed my life and made me the man I am today.

Have you ever tossed a pebble into the pool of life just to watch the ripples flow out from the splash? I ask you, the reader, what kind of rock are you tossing into the pool of life? This is cause and effect to its fullest. The rocks I have tossed over the years still have ripples flowing. I believe the ripples keep going for eternity. Look at what it did to my dear old cousin Dean. And look at what it did to my victim. Even my grandchildren are still feeling the effects of my actions of thirty years ago. Way before they were even born, the ripples continue go on and on. I will speak more about this later in the book. Please continue on the journey with me.

Building a Reputation

Back to 1987. My life consisted of getting high and making a name for myself in prison. I started hustling pot for this old-timer. I made enough money to feed my addiction. Old Tony was quite the character. What I didn't know was that I was being used. I would collect the money for the dope. Tony had the connections to keep the supply going, or so I thought. Tony had this personality problem. He thought he was this big Italian gangster. He thought that he was connected with the mob. As time passed, he was exposed.

There is one thing about time that will never change. It will prove you or it will expose you. The sad thing about living a life that is a lie— it will always catch up with you. Tony got caught up in the "I am this and I am that." Come to find out, old Tony was nothing but a two-bit con man. I found out that he was in debt to some heavy hitters. When I found this out, I went to him and demanded the money that he owed me. I told him that I would take him off the yard. I gave him one week to get my money, which was a mistake. It wasn't but two days later I found myself sitting in a transport van heading to the penitentiary. I found out Tony was a rat too.

The Nebraska State Penitentiary looked real menacing with all the guard towers around it. I thought that I was being promoted to the big time as the van pulled in. I stepped off the van and took my property to the housing unit I was assigned to. I knew a few good dudes that were serving time in the penitentiary, and it didn't take me long to get hooked back up with the like-minded folks. One thing about prison, there is always dope and a way to get anything you want.

My first week at the pen was an awakening. As I walked around the housing unit to go to the weight pile and exercise, I noticed that these two guys were circling each other. I recognized right away that they both had knives taped to their hands. As they tried to stab each other, you could hear the oohs and ahs from the crowd that was gathering. I just kept on walking. I learned a long time ago to mind my own business. Later on, I found out that Fast Freddy was trying to reclaim his punk from another inmate.

There are a few things that I learned from the old-timers over the years. I will never forget what Curley Wolf had taught me. It has kept me safe for a long time. He told me, "There are three things you need to know that will help you. First, mind your own business. Second, do your own time. Third, keep your mouth shut." Curly Wolf (RIP) was a good old convict. He also taught me that "You can never tell the depth of the well by the size of the handle on the pump." In other words, you cannot judge a book by its cover. Do not judge people by their appearance; try to get to know them first.

I settled in and got a job working in the woodshop. I learned to make chair frames. I would go to the shop during the day and play poker in the evening. My weekends were spent getting high and playing poker. This would be the normal routine for a few months. While working in the shops, I met a lifer named Yippee. I discovered that he had the same ideologies as I did. It didn't take long for us to put a petition together. We wanted to start a religion that was called

Asatru and have it added to the religious roster as a recognized religion. This was a religion known to be popular in the federal prison system; it was also deeply mired in racism, or what we called racial pride.

I couldn't believe how simple it was to get started. It eventually grew to a nice size. We had about twenty solid white guys assembled. We obtained a little piece of land behind the shops so we could hold our religious rites. We were also allowed a firepit and wood. We would assemble for weekly land days in which we would hold blots, or what are called religious rites.

It was nice to be on the land and hold up a horn. I would give hails to the gods and goddesses of my ancestors, the same gods and goddesses my forefathers believed in. It didn't take me long to rise to the top. I became a Gothi, which is like a teacher, an elder, and a leader all put together.

There was one thing that I did to ensure that only the strong were allowed in the kindred. I would check their courage. I used to corner a prospect in the library, and then when we were in a blind spot, I would intentionally bump into him. I would say, "What the hell's your problem, punk?" I got in their face, hoping they would rear up and fight. Many lowered their heads and copped put, even when it was not their fault. Those guys were not allowed in. But you take the guy who reared up and wanted to fight. He would be the one who made the cut. He was allowed to learn the kindred ways. I needed to be certain of who I kept company with, especially if I was going to bleed with him. To get into the kindred, one must take a blood oath. The mentality was "blood in and blood out." This would be something that would haunt me years later, when I renounced my ties with all the hate groups, i.e., the white supremacists.

It's been almost thirty years since I helped start the first kindred at the Nebraska State Penitentiary. Now there are kindreds in every prison within the Nebraska Department of Corrections, and every one of them is going strong.

I ran into a man recently who asked me what became of the man who assisted him in becoming racially aware, the man who woke him up from the slumber of ignorance that was killing his race.

I was that man who woke him up. Now I am the man who tries to show him that I was wrong in many ways. I did not know I had that much influence or power over people.

3

Nothing Has Changed

From the spring of 1987 to the day that I paroled in the spring of 1990, my time did not change. I filled my days with shooting dope, lifting weights, and preparing myself for release, which meant I was gearing up to get out and make up for lost time.

I was celling with a childhood friend before I was paroled. I was in contact with his sister Deborah through letters. I told her I that was taking applications for an Ole Lady. This hooked her. She was working as a waitress/bartender at a local strip club in Omaha, which was right up my alley.

I had my dear mother and her best friend since childhood, Ellie (Aunt Ellie), pick me up on the day that I paroled. On the way back to Omaha, we stopped at a restaurant which was located at Linoma Beach. This was the lake where Ma and Pa and Aunt Ellie's family had their camping trailers at. I spent quite a few weekends there. The steak that I ordered was great, but I felt out of place for some odd reason. To this day, I look back and wonder why I didn't feel as if I belonged to society anymore. I had that eerie feeling that I did not fit in anywhere.

I talked Juki into bringing Tommy and Holly over to the house so I could see them. I also had intentions of getting Juki alone so I could get laid. Three years was a huge amount of time to go without sex. This was a sign that I would not pay heed to. Here she was cheating on her current husband with me. Didn't this happen before? I didn't care that she cheated on me. All I wanted was to do was get laid.

Three days had passed since I walked out of the penitentiary on parole, and the phone rang at Mom's house around 2:30 am. Mom woke me up and told me my parole officer was on the phone. I paroled to Mom's house and was living in the basement. They had a nice little setup for me.

I said, "Hey, what's up?" This person didn't sound like my parole officer. It was Deb, my childhood friend's sister. I told her that in the last letter I had written her, I would be at Mom's house if she wanted to hook up.

Deb wanted to come over and pick me up. She just got off work and was higher than a kite. I said, "Hell yeah, come on over and get me." My life was never to be the same again. I knew that within days, I would be getting high.

A lot of men in prison say that they will change and that they miss their kids. They also say their kids are the most important things in their life. I was one of those men who said they were never going to leave their children again once they got out of prison. It didn't take me long to forget about those words.

A man who is all about self-gratification is a man who is addicted to something. No matter if his intentions are good or bad. They always end up being about him. He will always fulfill his needs at any cost. A lot of men don't think about the price they have to pay until it's too late. I was no different. I was going to a pay the ultimate price again—my freedom.

It wasn't but a few days spent with Deb, and I was back to my selfish ways. My family took a back seat to my addiction again. Time with my kids turned into a weekend here and a weekend there. All my time was spent with Deb. I was back on the meth and drinking like a fish.

It turned out that Deb had a better dope connection than I did. I went back to spending all my time at the strip clubs and biker bars. Only this time, my girl worked at the strip club. She used to dance but got too old to shake her moneymaker all night long. But she could still hustle.

For the next few months, I would take Deb to work at the strip club where she was waitressing. I would drink for free, and I would sell meth out of the bar. I was on a fast track to failure.

I knew I was a mess. My little sister was getting married, and she asked me to take my elderly grandmother to the reception hall. I knew that they didn't want me around the party bus. Everyone was going to be partying on the double-decker bus. They were going to take a slow route around the city.

I loaded up my nose with a line of meth and did what I do best: be by myself. At the reception, I had a bottle of gin. I kept it in Deb's purse so when we would get cups of soda, I would load it up with gin. Between drinks, we would take turns going to the bathroom or the car and snorting lines of meth. Once again, all was well in my warped world.

One thing I distinctly remember at the wedding, my mother asked me to dance with her one time. She was worried about me, and I think she knew I was on my way back to prison. She wanted to have a memory that was good instead of bad. I remember feeling the love and security every time I was around my mom. This would be something that I would miss for decades.

Over the years, I would occasionally think about those times and those feelings. I sometimes wondered why I would choose the paths in life that would always lead me from the people and things that meant the most to me. *Addiction is a coldhearted bitch!*

I ended up marrying Deb within a few months of knowing her. I broke another promise to myself—the one where I said I would not get into any relationship for at least one year after release. This relationship was built around getting high and insecurity on both our parts.

I would get my kids on the weekend and try to be a dad, which was hard. I never knew how to be a dad in the first place. The dope would always become more important to me than my own kids. As the days rolled on by, I would see less and less of the kids.

My ex-wife, Juki, went to my parole officer and tried to get me thrown back into prison for not paying my child support. I would despise her after that, and out of that spite, I would not pay her anything.

It wasn't long before I received a Driving While Intoxicated charge. Deb had quit her job, and life was a mess. We ended up moving in with my folks. We lived in their basement, and my son Joe loved it because Dad was back at home.

Not only had Deb and I moved in, but we had Deb's daughter, Linda, with us. Here I was, trying to be a father to Linda, and I couldn't even be one to my own kids.

As the weeks rolled by, my addiction would get worse. I got a job at a packing house, and it would be enough to allow Deb and me to get an apartment in South Omaha.

One thing about working in a packing house, there were always good uppers to be had. When times got tough and our drug connections would dry up, I could always count on one of my coworkers to have something. I would be getting high on meth or white crosses during the day and smoking pot at night to come down. At one point, we scored some Thorazine from Deb's uncle. We would split a pill in half and come down, only to wake up the next day and start again.

It didn't take long before I would get hurt at work and go on workman's comp. I fell down some greasy stairs at the packing plant and hurt my back. The doctor at the hospital prescribed some pain pills, and I loved pain pills. I would love anything that took away the loneliness that I carried around in my heart. I just never talked about it or ever told anyone.

I spent the days getting high and selling meth in the strip clubs. It was great to have a wife who loved to go to the strip clubs with me. These were her friends and the people that she had worked with for years. All I did was waste away.

At one of my doctor's visits, I was told that the blood work had shown that my liver functions were real bad. They wanted to do some tests. I declined. I knew that it was a result of my drinking and drug use. I had been back on the needle, and neither Deb nor anyone else knew it. There are some things an addict won't do, and admitting he has a problem is one of them. I would sit around snorting meth with Deb and our friends and talk bad about addicts using syringes. "Low lives," I would say. I was a mess.

I hid my needle use real well, but I became the thing that I despised the most—a hypocrite. It didn't take me long to go back to what I knew—pulling robberies. Deb's father-in-law was in town and had shown me a Mossberg 500, a short-barrel shotgun that he had in the trunk of his car. I stole it out of his trunk before he left town. It didn't take me long to have it in my possession.

I was not working and was hurting for some money. I was supposed to sell the shotgun at the corner bar, but instead, I turned it into a reason to party. I ran into Deb's brother. He didn't want to buy the gun, so instead we shot up some dope. One thing I have a hard time wrapping my mind around is how I always had money to get high or drunk but never to put gas in the car or take the kids to a movie (not that I would have taken them). I was a piece of work.

The only vision an active addict has is the next score, at any cost. I was no different. I left the bar, drove around South Omaha until I found a quick score, and staked it out. I went in, stuck the shotgun in the clerk's face, and had him fill the brown paper sack with what was in the register. I also took the customer's money. I didn't care. I ran out and got into the car that I parked behind the store. I drove for two blocks and hid in an alley behind a friend's house. I laughed every time I saw a cop car drive by.

After an hour had passed, I made my way to the Quickie Mart a mile down the road. I filled the gas tank up and bought a carton of cigs. Then I proceeded to the next gas station that I planned to rob. I knew this would be a bigger score. After that, I could lie low for a while.

I pulled into the all-night gas station, and I knew they had a stash of money. It was Saturday night, and the score was always big on weekends. I took the gun out of the coat and pointed it at the clerk. I had him fill the sack up with everything that he had in the safe. It looked like a nice sack of money, and I ran to the car. It was an old beat-up Maverick that ran like a turtle with constipation.

I no sooner pulled out of the driveway than a cop car was pulling in for a coffee break. My luck sucked! I took off, and the cop followed in fast pursuit. I made it down the street a couple of blocks and parked behind a house. I hid the car behind it in a driveway. I laid low for about an hour. I finally stepped out of the car and put the gun and money into the trunk. I didn't see any cop cars, so I decided to slowly drive off and try to make my way back home.

I didn't even make it two blocks before I found myself in an intersection, surrounded by what I guess to have been around ten cop cars. I looked around me, and all that I saw was a whole lot of guns pointed at me. They yelled for me to get my hands up and step out of the car. I knew it was all over at that point. I was mad at myself because I put the gun in the trunk. I didn't want to go back to prison. I wanted to die right then and there.

As I stood there getting handcuffed, I heard one officer tell another that I was the same perp that he had busted a few months earlier. If he was a betting man, he would put his money on me returning to prison. Everyone was seeing it but me. Deep inside, I knew I was on a fast track to total failure. It was a long ride to the all-so-familiar city jail.

That All-So-Familiar Sound

With a loud bang, the big heavy steel door shut behind me once again. There I was, back in the county jail and on my way to the state pen. It took *about* four months for me to get my parole revoked and to be sentenced for three more counts of armed robbery. I was told that if I pled guilty to the three counts of armed robbery, I would only receive five to ten years and that the three counts would be run together. This would give me a concurrent sentence that would total eight to seventeen years. However, the judge had other plans and ran the three five- to ten-year sentences consecutively. This meant that I had fifteen to thirty years added to the original three- to seven-year sentence, giving me a new total of eighteen to thirty-seven years. I was expected to serve all of my time at the Nebraska State Penitentiary.

Within a few weeks, I was transferred to the Diagnosis and Evaluation Center in Lincoln, Nebraska. I hated that cramped and overcrowded place. It seemed that everything ran super slow there. It would end up being a long wait. I took the initiative to use a threatening manner in all I did. The staff attempted to transfer me out of there fast. No luck! I laughed at the system and the staff they had in place. They tried to make me follow all their rules. I was having none of that. I had an expensive wedding ring on my finger that I knew would be confiscated, but I also knew that I would be able to get top dollar for it when I got back to the penitentiary. So I wrapped it in a piece of plastic and put it in the bank (my rectum).

Once the van pulled into the entrance of the state penitentiary, I knew it would be a very long time before I would see the streets of South Omaha again. Here it was, one year since I paroled out, and I was back in. I felt really embarrassed and knew, once I walked out onto the yard, I would here the ridicule from the guys.

All the fellas were there to give me the blues about returning to prison. They had all the comments about seeing me on the news and not been gone long and how I must have missed the chow. But the one that bothered me the most was "You couldn't make it out there."

I went to see my case manager to see about how much time I would have to pull on these eighteen to thirty-seven years. What he told me was not what I wanted to hear. I was to pull fifteen straight calendars without hope for parole. This was devastating to me, and all I could think about was how that judge screwed me.

One lesson I would learn later in life would be accountability. Unfortunately, it would take me years to learn it. Right now, I did not have any accountability, and I would not look at the fact that I put myself back in prison. From my selfish standpoint, the system let me down. It was always someone else's fault anyway.

I took back my rightful place as leader of the kindred. All I would do was spread hate and discontent. One thing I did was hate on the Christians and the Jews. I was so against religion and their Jew God. I let everyone know it.

One thing you see in prison is the guy that turns to Christianity as soon as the door shuts closed behind him. Then as soon as he gets on parole or out of prison, he forgets all about God and starts to, once again, worship drugs. I have seen it over and over throughout the years. Or you will see the guy that goes to church and carries the Bible around preaching, only to go back to his cell and get high and have sexual relations with his punk (hypocrisy at its finest).

I thought about all the years that I would have to pull, and I was pissed at the judge. I divorced Deb. It was what she wanted. Hell, I wasn't even settled in yet and she gave all my clothes away. All I could think about was how another man was screwing my woman, wearing my good engineer boots, and putting on my favorite leather jacket.

We go through life worrying about all the things that we have no control over. Why do we not give any thought to all the things that we do have control over? It would take me years to learn that lesson.

A Way Out

I was sitting behind the housing unit and smoking a cigarette when the garbage truck pulled up. It was there to empty the dumpsters that were behind the chow hall. I looked at the big truck and then up and down the fence line. A smile came over my face. I had found a way out.

The next day, I was sitting there pondering the situation when a friend of mine, Crow, who was doing life, came up to me and asked what I was looking at. I mentioned that there was a weak area in the fence line and I was wondering if that garbage truck would make it through or knock enough of it down. I needed to make it over the outside fence. I knew I could trust my bro Crow, especially when it came to keeping his mouth shut. Talking about an escape was a conversation that was kept on the QT.

I found out that I wasn't the only one checking the truck out. He told me that he and a couple of other convicts were planning to take over the garbage truck and didn't want me to mess their plans up. I was like, "Cut me in or I do it myself." Crow said he would get back to me.

A day later, Nose comes up talking about it and who was involved. I was in, and I would meet the rest of the guys later. I was asked if I could drive. I was like, "Hell yeah, I will drive." That was the plan, and over the next few months, we would all get together and fine-tune the foolproof plan. As you probably already know, and I would find out later, nothing is foolproof.

There were a few other guys involved—the Old Man PK, TC, and Spat. As the day that we planned to take off came closer, a few guys got cold feet and pulled out. We had a lot to do, like get light bulbs, flammable liquid, and also make sure that we had sharp shanks. It would take a few trips from the plate shop to get the flammables ready. We had a couple of gallon jugs stashed and ready. I also had Clay bring me the honing block from the Hobby Center so TC and I could sharpen the knives that our buddy had made us.

I had one of my kinsmen from the kindred, Jimbo, do a rune pull for me. I wanted to see if the Norns were in favor of the escape or not. Was Lady Fortuna with me? The pull was negative, and it told me to back up off the attempt. But as a man of my word, I wouldn't and couldn't. In prison and in life, a man's word is his bond, and I gave my word.

I moved into Wizard's cell. He wanted in and we were bros, so we celled together. We were getting ready to be on the run and needed a game plan to make it out of the state. I was shooting a lot of speed every day, and I felt no pain. I do not know how I was even coherent enough to help put a plan together, but I did.

Don't You Know Who I Am?

About one month before we were to escape, I left the cell, and for some reason I forgot my cigarettes in the cell. I saw my friend Billy walking down the sidewalk in front of the cell house where I was sitting and said, "Hey, Billy, you got a smoke on you?"

He said, "Sure don't, Big T." His buddy was with him, and I asked him if he had a smoke I could get until I got back into the cell house. He said no. Then he pulled out a pack of smokes and passed one to Billy.

Of course, I said to him, "What the hell, what's up with your friend, Billy?"

This guy said to me, "F——k you, man. I am not giving you anything."

I said to him, "Look, motherf——er, I told you. I left mine in the cell. But if you want to be a smart-ass, I will beat the shit out of you right now." I took off chasing him all the way to the T-Dorm, which was a dorm for lower security men and had a gate that I couldn't get through. This guy cussed at me and called me every name in the book. I told him I would get him.

I waited until he was at work. I knew he would be on the big yard at noon. All my guys were out there. They knew what was going to go down. I opened the *back of my TV up and pulled out this ten-inch knife that I had made in the plate* shop. I put it in my waistband and waited for this smart-ass to come by.

Here he came, slowly walking up the pathway. I stepped out and got him cornered behind cell house no. 2. He saw me pull out the shank and dropped to his knees.

"Please don't kill me!" he cried out. As I started to swing the blade, aiming for his neck, I stopped. I wasn't sure why, but there was something in his eyes that stopped me.

I said to him, "You don't know who I am, do you?"

He said, "I didn't, but Billy told me that you were Big T. I didn't know who you were. I am sorry."

I told him to look at all the guys standing over behind cell house no. 4. Those were my guys. I explained to him that he was going to go to each one of them and apologize to them for disrespecting me.

One thing about a scared man in prison, he will do about anything to get out of trouble, and this guy was in deep crap. He went to each man and apologized for the disrespect. He couldn't believe that he almost lost his life over a cigarette. It wasn't about the cigarette. He later learned that it was about his smart mouth and his lack of not knowing the Convict Code.

He tried to give me a carton of smokes, and I declined. I told him that he didn't owe me anything. He learned a lesson. I was getting ready to escape, and I did not need any more attention on myself.

I looked around and saw a lot of guards on the yard, so I decided to hide the shank. I couldn't get back into the unit so I could hide it close to the normal stash spot. In prison, there is always a stash spot somewhere. As I walked by the unit, I saw a spot that was close to the cell house. I thought that this would be an easy extraction when I needed the shank. I was by Housing Unit no. 4, and I sat on the stairwell. I realized that I could bury the shank under the stairs. There was a mound of loose dirt that the ground squirrels had built by cleaning their holes out. I leaned in and slid the shank into the dirt and marked it. Only I would know where it was at.

A couple of weeks later, the eve before I was going to escape, I went to the stairwell to retrieve the knife. I couldn't get it out of the ground. The ground squirrels had piled more dirt over it. It had rained, and with the hot temperatures, the mound was rock-hard. "What am I going to do now?" I had to come up with another shank fast.

I went to Jimmy T. I told him that I needed a piece of steel. And he just happened to have one. It was hidden in a tube of toothpaste. I took it to the cell and cleaned it up.

One thing about silver linings and ripple effects is that it may be years before you discover them and the meaning of the results of your actions. I don't mean to get ahead of myself, but I need to tell you about the guy I was going to stab over disrespecting me. Well, he showed up in my life twenty-five years later, and I took the opportunity to thank him. You need to understand that the shank that I would have used to escape with (the big sharp one that I buried under the stairwell) if I used it, the guard would have probably died. I would have ended up on death row.

The beauty about silver linings is they show themselves in their own time, but you have to look for them. Who would have thought that if this man didn't do what he did that day, the end result of my actions would have been worse than they were. *In a roundabout way, twenty-five years later, I am in gratitude to the man with the smart mouth and to the ground squirrels.*

4

What Have I Become?

August 31, 1991, I woke up and got high on some speed. It was time to get the courage up for what was about to go down. I looked at Wizard and asked him if he was ready to rock and roll. We took a bunch of black pepper that we brought out of the kitchen and spread it all over the cell. We didn't want the dogs to get a good scent in case the guards used them to track us down.

I also left a smart-ass note to the warden that said, "See you later. I don't like it here anymore." Then I took the shank that I had worked on, the one I got from Jimmy T. I placed it in my waistband as we headed out the cell door.

We all met at the stairwell to go over our plans. Everyone showed up. One of the guys that backed out came up and wanted to hang around. I said to him in a nice way that he needed to get his coward ass away from me. In hindsight, he had more testicular fortitude than I had, because he backed out and I should have, but that good old social mirror dictated my decisions.

Everything looked good, except the trash truck was late because of a flat tire. We saw Crow's buddy drive by in the pickup truck. We knew the guns were inside the pickup truck and were outside the fence awaiting our arrival. Two of the guys took the bag that was full of Molotov cocktails and got into position. The plan was to throw Molotovs at the gun tower as we drove the garbage truck through a weak spot in the fence line. It happened to be right under the guard tower.

I was asked to drive the truck, so I didn't carry any flammable liquids. My job was to secure the driver's side of the truck and drive.

THE RIPPLE EFFECT

As the truck pulled up behind the kitchen to pick up the garbage, PK, Wizard, and I walked up behind the dumpsters as they were getting ready be hooked up and emptied into the truck. I tried to figure out why Red showed up for work. This only meant two things: someone told him about our plans, and the guard would have to stay in the truck. Now we would have to extract the guard from the truck.

All I could think about was, *Crap, here we go*. I walked around the back of the truck while Wizard and PK went around to the passenger side. I heard PK yell for Wizard to get the guard that was escorting the truck. As I came up the driver's side, I saw the escort take off running. He was yelling as he held his hands to his face. I knew Wizard had thrown fluid in his face to scare him.

We had made a pact that no one would get hurt unless it was necessary. That was soon to be broken. PK was in the truck. He entered through the passenger side door, which was unlocked. As I came up the driver's side, I looked into Red's eyes. I gave him the death stare. I am really at good giving someone the death stare. I saw the fear in his eyes. I made it to the driver's door and pulled on the handle. Nothing happened! I saw PK and the guard struggling with each other inside the cab of the truck. I stepped onto the running board to reach in and unlock the door. All I could smell was the flammable liquid that was in the Molotov cocktails. I wondered why he had the fluid with him. As I stepped back down to pull on the handle to open the door, I heard the engine stop.

Before I could get the truck door opened, the guard threw the keys out the truck's window. They landed in the tall weeds that overran the perimeter of the fence line. There was no way to know where the hell they landed. I knew from our information that the guard had another ignition key. It was on a separate keychain that was attached to his belt. The only problem we had was that we didn't know that the guard had a flat tire on the truck that morning and had to swap keys. Since it happened to be a holiday weekend, the guard only carried the garage keys with him and not the extra ignition key.

The smell of the flammable liquid was very strong. I knew right away PK had tossed some on the guard. As I stepped onto the running board, the guard kicked me. I took ahold of his leg as I fell backward, and I dragged him out of the truck. As we both fell to the ground, I stabbed him with the shank. I told him to lie still and not to be a hero. As I was taking the keys off his belt, PK had gotten out of the truck and made his way to where I was. I was holding the guard down as I removed the keys off his belt. I felt my hand start to sting. I realized that PK was right next to me. He was stabbing the guard. In his frenzy, he ended up stabbing me through the hand.

I got the keys, and I climbed into the truck. I started to go through every key on the ring, but nothing was working. As I was going through the keys a second time, I noticed PK getting into the truck. He lit up a smoke and said, "That will teach him."

I said, "You crazy bastard. There is flammable liquid all over this truck and you want to smoke?" What I didn't realize was that the guard was rolling around on the ground. PK had set him on fire.

I saw the hood of the truck start to open. The other guards were running to the truck. They started to disable it, but it was already disabled from the guard tossing the keys to the fence line. We are surrounded and were told to get out of the truck. As I stepped out of the truck, I saw the guard lying there. He was surrounded by inmates. One inmate had his hand on the guard's back while another was holding a shirt that looked like it had been burned. Only then did I realize that the guard had been set on fire. I didn't know what to think. I was numb. What the hell did I get myself into?

As I was handcuffed behind my back, I looked away from the truck and saw about three hundred inmates standing around, most of them with a look of shock on their faces. I saw one of my bros, Gidge. He was standing there. I said, "Nice knowing you, bro." I knew my life was over and I would rot away in the hole.

I was escorted to turnkey, a building that was the hub of the prison. As soon as I was placed into a holding cell, I realized that I was bleeding. Every time I squeezed my hand to make a fist, blood shot out of the wound. I was handcuffed with my hands behind my back. I stayed that way for quite a few hours while the prison staff tried to figure out what the hell had just happened inside their prison.

As I looked out the window of the holding cell, I saw PK. He was being held in an adjacent holding cell. He looked at me and smiled. I asked him what was up, and he proceeded to tell me how he doused the guard and lit him up. I felt sick and that my life had come to an end. I was at the lowest point that my life had ever been. All I could think about was to hell with everything. I continued to squeeze my hand and shoot streams of blood onto the walls. I couldn't believe PK stabbed me through my finger as I was trying to get the keys from the guard.

The guards walked into the holding cell. They had a nurse with them. She looked at my hand and told the guards that I wasn't hurt. She then took a pair of tweezers and yanked a hoop earring out of my nose. Imagine a bull with a ring in its nose, which was what I looked like. It was as if the nurse was getting some satisfaction by afflicting pain on me. Hindsight was 20/20. I knew that all the staff looked upon me with hate and discontent. That was the new norm and how it would be for the next three decades. *I was enemy number one*, only to be known as the infamous Tom Fleming.

I saw Wizard being escorted up the stairs. He was being taken to a different part of the prison. He was also surrounded by a bunch of investigators, so I knew he was about to be interrogated. After a few hours passed by, I was chained up with leg irons and a waist chain with handcuffs attached to it. Then the guard put the come-a-long on me (this is a pair of handcuffs attached to a long chain with a hoop at the end) so he could keep me held close, like a dog on a leash.

It was a long walk from turnkey to the Control Unit. I was forced to walk barefooted. It was about a two-city-block distance. Here I was, barefooted, in chains, with a "screw the world" look upon my face. As I did the shuffle to the hole, I saw a lot of guards combing the yard with metal detectors. I also saw that they had Molotov cocktails and a few homemade knives in their hands.

I wondered if my bros got away or if they got cuffed up as well. I knew it wouldn't be long before the prison snitch system would kick in and give up any and all information they could get ahold of. It didn't matter if the information was true or not. One thing about prison I noticed over the years, and most of the guards will agree with me, is that most of the information they obtain is because someone told them.

Into the Belly of the Beast

South 40. That was a title the old-school convicts called it. The prison staff called it the Control Unit. I called it home. I learned a long time ago to have the attitude that *where I lay my head is home.* I believe that is a name of a Metallica song. The segregation unit at the state penitentiary would be my home for the next ten and a half years. As I walked into the old building that was built in the late forties or early fifties, I noticed it was all bars, and it had the old hand-operated levers. You knew you were in the old-school aura when all the doors and cells were still operated by hand levers. The whole building smelled of urine and feces. My thoughts were scrambled, and I was numb.

I was escorted to a cell on the A-side. This side of the unit held eighteen cells. The other side, B-side, also held eighteen cells. I was led down the walkway. It would be the first of many while still attached to that al-so-familiar dog leash. As I was surrounded by six guards, all chained up, it had me thinking that I looked like Hannibal Lecter. As I backed into the seven-by-nine-foot cell, I went slowly. The leg restraints were so tight that they were digging into my ankles with every step that I took. Once I was far enough into the cell, the guard fed the lead chain (leash) through the hatch. The hatch was a little hole in the steel door; its purpose was to allow the guard to pass your food tray through it. It also served as a barrier between the inmate and staff. It was made of thick steel and made a great deal of noise when slammed shut with force. It would soon become my worst enemy, or I should say the best tool that the guards would use to get me to react.

One thing about a cell in the segregation unit, it had a night-light that was very bright, and it never went out. The regular lights and the night-light were florescent. Because the light never went out, it played tricks on a person's mind after a period. It was very hard to sleep in those conditions. I got used to sleeping with a stretched-out sock wrapped around my head to cover my eyes.

The first few nights seemed like psychological torture. There was an intercom system within the cell. It was mounted inside a steel cage on the wall. There was a guard continuously on the intercom. He yelled at me all night long. This went on for about five days. He would say the same thing over and over: "If he dies, I hope I get to pull the lever that will fry your ass. I can't wait to see you fry in that electric chair!" This would be the attitude of every employee in the prison system, and it would last for decades. This negative attitude toward me exists to this day in a few of the guards that still work within the prison system.

Part of me wanted to die in that electric chair, and part of me wanted to live just so I could be that man that said, "You couldn't break me and never will." As I paced the cell floor, which was but four steps each way, I said to myself, "Man up. Man up, boy! You have at least ten years to do in this hellhole." I did a lot of pacing in the cells of South 40. I wore out a lot of shoes over the next thirteen years.

I would soon learn that the hole (segregation) was a world like no other. Can you imagine spending twenty-three hours of the day locked up behind a steel door in a seven-by-nine-foot room that was all brick? The only time you were allowed out of the cell was for one hour a day, five days a week, for exercise purposes only. Some days you hope for a medical pass so you could walk across the yard. The distance from the segregation unit to the medical building was around one and a half to two blocks, and you walked in full restraints. This was known as the shuffle. It didn't take me long to get used to walking around in leg restraints, having a chain wrapped around my waist with handcuffs attached to it. It was usually called a waist chain or a belly chain.

For the next several years, I was classified as full restraint status. This meant that anytime I was out of my cell, I was to be placed in full restraints. I was in full restraints when I went to the shower. I was also in full restraints when I went to the yard to exercise. The norm for me was to not show any discomfort when the restraints were put on too tight. When I would go to the little exercise yard, the guard would put the leg restraints around my ankles. He would tighten them up until they pinched my skin. Then he would give them a click or two and smile. My defiant attitude never allowed me to show any pain. I would shuffle out to the yard, and I would start to jog as the guards would look on. By the time I would come back into the cell, my ankles would be blistered and bloody. They would comment on how the restraints fit me like a glove, and then I would give them a smile. Only my smile looked more like an evil sneer.

There was a nutcase whose name was Fat Chuck. He lived in the cell next to me. The guards would reward him with tobacco if he pounded on the cell wall all night long. I wasn't in that cell but two days when I heard him ask the guard for some more smokes or he wasn't going to keep me up day and night anymore. The old-school cons tried to tell Fat Chuck to not mess with me, but he wouldn't listen. I was at my limit with him, and I had a couple of metal clips that a guy slid under my cell door. They were off some heavy-duty legal binders. I took them and started digging all the filler out between the cement bricks that separated our cells. I didn't realize that there was rebar in between the walls, and I knew that I wasn't going to get to him right away.

I did not know what I was going to do with all the cement I had dug out of the wall. I ended up washing it out of the cell and into the hallway. My bro came by to clean the run. It was his job, so he cleaned it up for me.

He said, "What are you going to use to fill the cracks in with, Big T?"

I said, "I have some mashed potatoes that I saved from dinner. I was going to use that as filler. I don't need the guards discovering that I was trying to get into Fat Chuck's cell."

There is a mind trip that a person goes through every day in solitary confinement. It is hard to explain. There are a lot of emotional ups and downs that the day brings, especially as the months and years pass by. I knew I was enemy number one, and the hate upon the guards' faces showed it. I would eventually figure out how a lot of these guys doing long-term segregation got by. They stayed numb. The psychotropic drugs were the answer, or at least I thought they were. I conned the doctor into giving me Valium, and I would trade it for some better drugs, like Xanax or Klonopin.

I knew a few guys that had good connections to score drugs, and I learned how to trade and barter. My kinsmen that lived in general population were helping me get good weed smuggled into the Control Unit. I was put on flammable material restriction, which meant that I couldn't have a lighter or any Roll-Rite tobacco. The prison used to give out free tobacco to the guys in segregation every week. I still received tobacco; it was given to me by other men in the unit. Once the guards were aware of this, there was a big push to make us suffer and not be able to smoke in the segregation unit. None of the other cons were too happy when the administration took smoking out of the segregation unit.

If there is one thing to know about a convict, it is this—he will find a way to get what he wants, sooner or later. I was very fortunate to have a second cousin, Wolfgang, working in the legal library, and another, the Kid, working in the canteen. This enabled me to keep smoking and stay high for years. If I wasn't getting contraband from the library, I was getting it smuggled in from the canteen. The Kid would put coffee, gum, tobacco, and weed into a bag of cookies then reseal it.

One thing I learned was how to smuggle tobacco into the segregation unit. When I would go to the legal library, I would pick up a package and find a way to get it past the guards. Being an addict, I learned that I had to be clever and go to any length to get high. Smoking tobacco was no different; it kept me sane. At least that's what I believed at the time.

I would go to the legal library every week to see if I had a package waiting for me. Or I would hope that another guy that I got along with had a package waiting for him, and I would bring it back. What I didn't like was the simple fact that to get the package back safely, I had only had two ways that would work. One was making a slipknot on a piece of dental floss. The dental floss would be tied to a Band-Aid. Once I received the package, I would slip the string around it and cinch it up, then place it in my waistband until I returned to the Control Unit. Once back in the Control Unit and in position to be strip-searched, I would wait until the guard would bend down to undo the leg shackles, then I would tape the package to the metal wall that separated us. The guard would not see the package of tobacco hanging there by a Band-Aid and dental floss. This maneuver lasted for years. The other way that was foolproof was to put it in the bank. This was what it was called in most prisons. It simply means to grease your anal cavity up with hair grease and then slip the shotgun shell-looking package up your butt, also known as *keistering* it.

The bullpen was located in the front part of the Control Unit. As you entered the building, you would have an option. You could turn left into the bullpen, depending if the gate was opened, or you could turn right and enter the office area. If you went straight to the back of the entryway, you would walk into the guard room where the intercom system was. The whole building was made up of steel bars. Every time I would leave the building, I would have to go through the bullpen area. This meant that I would be strip-searched twice, once leaving and once returning. Getting naked in front of numerous people day after day, year after year, is something that numbs you.

I went to great lengths to stay high and keep a supply of tobacco. I even paid other men to bring back my packages for me. This would end up causing problems. It is hard to find an honest prisoner. Many men in prison are drug addicts and alcoholics with no scruples. They will rip you off. They always have a song and a dance that they will try to sell you when they got caught. I have seen quite a few men get beat up pretty bad for taking what wasn't theirs. One thing I didn't understand very well was how one man wouldn't trust another man but would do business with him anyway. Then he would get mad when he was ripped off.

An Eye for an Eye

Going to the courthouse for the court proceedings was exhausting at times. I didn't like the abuse I would get verbally from the guards. This went on for weeks, and I had something in store for them. If I was to spend the rest of my life in prison and most of it in segregation, then what I had in store for them would not be idle threats. I was a violent man. To justify the violence, not that I had to justify anything to anyone, I would give them fair warning. I told them that if they kept treating me like a dog, I would bite like a dog.

    I did not do anything stupid that would allow the guards to suit up on me, which simply means they get into riot gear and use physical force upon you. They attempt to extract you from your cell and restrain you. I would always comply when they told me to cuff up. I had one guard that always slammed the steel hatch that I was fed through. It was only a matter of time until I paid him back. It seemed that every guard that rotated into the seg unit would take their shot at me, one way or the other. I did not look forward to the rotation, which took place every four months. Some guards would bid to get a rotation in the Control Unit. Their sole purpose was to dish out hate to the men that were stuck living behind the steel doors within the belly of the beast.

    I saved the money that was sent to me from a couple old convicts when they were released from prison. They knew that I would not have any means to buy myself any cosmetics or commissary from the canteen. I was never allowed a porter job. A porter job paid about thirty dollars a month. What I did was buy some headphones so I could listen to the radio that was piped into the cell via a plug in the wall. They didn't last long. I went outside for my one hour of recreation time, and when I returned to the cell, I found the wires from my headphones laying there on my bunk. Whoever shook down my cell took the time to yank the wires from the headphones. After a few times of getting my headphones broke by the guards, I quit buying them. I did remember who searched my cell every time that something was broken. I could not let the disrespect pass without applying any retaliation. *I had an "eye for an eye" attitude.* I never did get to pay the sergeant back for destroying my property. He rose up in rank and eventually became a warden.

    Men who are doing a lot of prison time love to go on travel orders. It doesn't matter if it is to an outside doctor or the courthouse. They all hope that an opportunity to escape might present itself. I was no exception. I filed a motion for a name change. I was granted a court hearing; the judge was going to hear my case. Back in those days, the prison staff would have to take you down to the courthouse. You had to appear in front of the judge for the hearing. I changed my name legally. I would now be now known as Tyrok Milosson. This was my Asatru name. When you're stuck in a cell, you need to try to break up the monotony. I did it by changing my name.

For almost three years, I went without headphones and a TV in the cell. I was on what we called Gilligan's Island. There was nothing in the seven-by-nine-foot cell but me. I was written up over one hundred times within a few years of being in the segregation unit. The guard that was slamming the hatch on my cell door did it one too many times. I used to throw food trays on him when he would spit in my food. He would spit in it right in front of me and then slam the food hatch. I would be placed on what they call Nutria-loaf, a combo of ground-up mush that looked bad and tasted even worse. I soon learned not to toss my food trays on him. I was losing too much weight by being on the loaf all the time.

I was paranoid every time I received a food tray. I would try to watch the guard when he was dishing the food out. I was told by one of my kinsmen that I had a meal delivered to me from the kitchen. The men in the Asatru kindred were cooking a special Yule meal. And they were sending me down some potatoes cooked with onions and also some pork that would be wrapped up in foil. When the meal was delivered to my cell, it was on a tray. The pork was laying in about an inch of liquid. I knew that the pork was in foil, so the liquid was suspicious. When the guard opened my hatch, he said, "Eat the ham. It looks really good." He walked away smiling. I immediately tossed the food into the toilet. I was pissed off. When the guard picked up the tray, he turned to face the bullpen area and nodded. He was confirming that I had eaten the meat. I heard the guards laughing in the office as soon as the guard delivered the empty tray to the kitchen area. At first, I could not believe that they pissed in my food. These state employees actually urinated in my food. My paranoia would last for years. I would always check my food trays for any signs of tampering.

One night, the hatch slammer was working, and he slammed the steel hatch really hard. He stood there smiling at me. I stood there with my hands covering my ears, waiting until the hatch was secure. Then he opened it up again and asked me if I wanted anything off the supply cart. He just asked me once, and I said some curse words to him. Then he said, "What are you going to do, stab me?"

I said, "Yes! Give me a sharp pencil."

He laid a sharp pencil on the steel hatch. I picked it up and placed it firmly in his stomach. I didn't feel any remorse. I didn't care about anything. The only regret I had was that I ended up with thirty days on sharp object restriction. For a long time, I was on one restriction or another. This lasted for the first few years of my segregation time.

Beat Me Down Like a Rabid Dog

A few months after I was admitted to the segregation unit, I was taken to the courthouse for a hearing. It was for my escape attempt. When I arrived at the courthouse and was sitting there waiting the judge to enter the room, the pills kicked in. I was higher than a kite. I took a couple of Xanaxes right before I left for the courthouse. As soon as the judge asked me if I waived my twenty-four-hour notice, I told him in a very impolite way that I didn't sign one. I also told him that the prison staff was a bunch of illiterates. I added a few more choice words. I made a spectacle out of myself and a mockery of the court. The judge told the prison staff to get me out of his courtroom. That was my twenty-four-hour notice.

As soon as I got back to the prison and returned to my cell, I was warned that I would pay for that outburst. I laughed at the guards in the manner that I usually did. That afternoon, my hatch came open. I was told to cuff up. I complied. I stuck my hands out of the open hatch in the cell door. It was a normal procedure so the cuffs could be placed over my wrists. Then I was asked to place my left ankle out the door so the leg irons could be placed over my ankles. I complied. Then the sergeant told the guard to rack the cell door, which simply means to open it. One thing about the old-style sliders is that the guard has to use a lever bar to operate the opening and closing of all the cell doors.

I stepped out of my cell and found myself surrounded by five guards. The sergeant stepped into my cell. He looked me in the eyes. Then he took out a cigarette and lit it up. I said, "Hell no, you just didn't do that?"

I was still oblivious to what was going to happen. The sergeant then tossed the lit cigarette into the commode and said to the other guards, "Get me an evidence bag. Fleming has been smoking in here."

I thought, *Okay, this is the payback for the crap I pulled at the courthouse when I was trying to embarrass them.* He retrieved the cigarette out of the commode, and he informed me that I was in violation of a few sanctions that were in the rule book. I said, "F*#k you!" I gave all of them my hardened "I will hurt you" stare.

I was told to step back into my cell. I complied. I placed my hands through the hatch when the cell door was halfway closed. Then I was told to place my left foot out of the cell door so the guard could remove the leg restraint that was around my ankle. I noticed the guard who had a hold of the long chain that was attached to my handcuffs was holding the chain tighter than normal. His stance was that of a man who was getting ready to wrestle a bull. Then the guard that was taking off my leg restraint grabbed my ankle. This had never happened before. As soon as he had a good grip on my ankle, he looked at the guard who was working the lever bar and said, "Okay."

The cell door opened a little and then started to close with force on my ankle. I yelled as I grabbed the door and said, "You're crushing my foot."

As soon as I grabbed the door to stop it from crushing my foot, the guard said, "He is resisting."

Right then, I knew I was just set up. The guard that was holding the long chain which was attached to my wrists tossed the chain through the hatch as the cell door came open. And the guard that held my foot grabbed my legs, and I was taken down to the floor. I was then dragged to the bullpen area that was out of sight from all eyes. Back in those days, there were no cameras that were recording things as they happened. I was still wearing the leg restraints, and what I like to call the dog leash was still around my wrists. As I lay on my stomach, one of the case managers grabbed and crossed my legs. He was pulling and bending them until they touched the small of my back. I felt something in my right knee give away. I cussed at him and asked if that was all he had. Then the other sergeant arrived on the scene. He took it upon himself to punch me in the face while I laid there in full restraints. It seemed that every guard from the prison was there. I kept seeing shadows move in and out of my peripheral vision.

I then said to the sergeant who was striking me in the face, "You hit like a little girl. My daughter can hit harder than that. You're a bitch."

That was not the brightest decision I had ever made. It pissed the sergeant off even more. He stood up and began to kick me in the face with his shiny-ass boots. I will never forget what those boots looked like. They are permanently etched in my memory.

I passed out for a few moments, and when I came to, I was being carried back to my cell. I asked the inmates who were watching out their little square windows which guard on my left side was wearing the shiny boots. I was placed back in my cell. The guards laid me on my stomach and started to remove the restraints from my body. I remember no more. I believe one of the guards delivered a blow that knocked me out again. When I woke up, I was all alone in the cell. I could hear the other convicts yelling my name. They were asking me if I was okay. I remember saying, "They messed me up really good."

When I stood up, the pain washed over me. It felt like I had been run over by a bus. I touched my face, and it felt swollen. I looked into the little four-by-four-inch plastic window that was in the back of the cell. This was a window that looked into the dark tunnel that ran behind the cells. It served as a somewhat mirror. I could barely see my face, and my eyes were almost swollen shut. I was a mess. I sat down and got mad at myself. I slipped up and let my guard down. I didn't see the setup happening until it was too late.

The next day, I was pulled out of my cell and escorted to the unit manager's office. He took photos of my face. Unbeknownst to me, one of the guards that was witness to the beating turned in a report. He went against his own coworkers. He said that excessive force was used against me, and it was retaliation for embarrassing them in the courtroom. He would have no part in it. I found out years later that the same guard was run out of the department by the "good old boy system." They didn't like the fact that he had turned them in. When I was asked what had happened to me, I just smiled and kept my mouth shut.

I was taken back to the courthouse. I had to go through the court procedures that didn't take place the day before. When I walked into the courtroom, the judge had a pow-wow with the guards that had escorted me into court. Then he asked me what happened to my face. I said, "I fell." I don't think that he believed me. I finished the court proceedings and was escorted back to the transport van. It was really quiet in the van, which was odd. The guards were usually quite cheery. Instead of going back to the prison, the van pulled up in front of the State Patrol Building. I was escorted inside the building and placed in a room. There sat three investigators from the State Patrol. I was asked to explain what had happened to me. I just looked at them. I wouldn't answer their question. Then I was asked to sit down. I did. They wanted to put wires on me for a polygraph test. They asked me one more time what had happened to me. I told them I had fallen in my cell. Then they asked if I would submit to the polygraph test. I said no. They kept telling me that they didn't believe me when I told them I had fallen in my cell. They also said that they were in possession of some information that informed them that I had been assaulted while in restraints. I laughed at them. I told them that I was not a snitch. I wouldn't tell on anyone. Not even a guard or my worst enemy.

I was transported back to the prison. On the way back, I informed the guards that just because I wouldn't give them up did not mean that I would not pay them back. I gave them fair warning. The war was on. It didn't take me long to start assaulting them one by one. Whether it was spitting blood in their face or hitting them with my fists when handcuffed. My motto was you beat me and treat me like a rabid dog, I will act like a rabid dog. This went on for a few months.

I was getting tired of planning and plotting every day. It was consuming my thoughts. Then I remembered what an old convict had told me one day before I tried to escape. He said, "If you go to the hole, when you get down there, screw up for a few months. Then lay your ass down, because it will show them that they won and are breaking your spirit." One thing I was always proud of was the fact that they threw everything they had at me, and they could not break me. I persevered through thirteen years of segregation, through all the isolation, and through all the head games. I would not allow my spirit to be broken.

I had seen many men enter the segregation unit and lose their minds. For some men, it would take weeks, some months, and others years. It always ended up badly for them. A few rubbed feces on themselves. I believe it was a cry for help. There were a couple of unfortunates who ended up committing suicide. They left in body bags. I witnessed three men kill themselves by asphyxiation at the state penitentiary. At the Tecumseh State Correctional Institution, I saw two more guys take themselves out of the game of life. They couldn't handle the solitude. Others would beat on doors or on their cell walls. *It was the norm to hear men screaming at no one yet yelling at everyone.* This happened at all hours of the day and night. I listened to a few men build relationships with unknown spirits, or what some would call gods and devils.

5

Don't Forget to Smell the Roses

One inmate that was doing a few years in the segregation unit with me had an aunt named Sherry he wanted me to write to. I was drawing on envelopes at the time. I would draw a lot of roses, butterflies, etc. This was a hustle for me. I didn't have any financial support at the time, so I would exchange an envelope with artwork on it for soap, shampoo, and more envelopes.

Sherry was a nurse. She would tell me about this rosebush she had planted in front of her house. She walked by it every day, awaiting its bloom. I sent her an envelope one day, and about a week later, I receive a letter from her. I opened the letter, and it said that on the previous Friday, she went into work, only to find out one of her patients, whom she cared for, had passed away overnight. As she was leaving work, it started to drizzle. Her car had a flat tire. To make matters worse, as soon as she got home, there was trash littered all over her front yard. The neighbors' dogs had gotten into the trash bags that were left out for the garbagemen to pick up. As she walked into the front door, she saw the letter lying in the foyer under the mail drop. On the envelope, she saw a beautiful red rose. She opened the envelope, and the letter simply said, "Have a nice day, and don't forget to stop and smell the roses." The roses! She forgot about the roses. She was so caught up in the crappy day that she spaced off the rosebush. She turned around and looked out the window. She realized that she had walked right by the blooming rosebush. She ran outside and sat down next to the roses. She began to cry. Sherry thanked me for making her day. That little rose on the envelope had a profound effect on her. I did that from a seven-by-nine-foot cell in segregation. This changed my life. *It gave my existence meaning.*

I started to see a reduction in the amount of misconduct reports I was receiving. I finally was lying low, and as a result, I was able to keep a TV in my cell. This was something that I would get addicted to, and the guards knew it. It was a bittersweet thing. The more I laid low and minded my own business, the more I was noticed. I started to get written up for violations that didn't happen, which would lead to my TV being taken away for various lengths of time. There were times when I discovered my cell had been searched and was in disarray. There was water all around the TV. The only way that could get there was if the guard searching the cell put it there. This had me checking the TV every day to see if the guard had poured water down the back of the TV again. Over the next thirteen years that I lived in the Segregation Unit, I would have not only water poured down my TV but also have the cords pulled from my headphones. I also had legal papers and photos from loved ones come up missing from time to time.

I somehow, in an odd way, got used to this treatment. I didn't agree with it, but I became numb to it. I believe if you treat a man as a dog, he will act like a dog. When I was poked with a stick, I would bite. One day I stopped biting. When I was poked with the stick, I smiled. I would not even bark. I was proud of the fact that I had laid my butt down long enough that the guards started to back off. The day-to-day abuse started to slow down.

Bare Bottom Blues

I love music! All music reaches the depth of my being. Growing up, I remember my paternal grandfather, George Fleming. He played the drums and the accordion. My father also played the accordion every now and then. He usually played it when he was drinking. He was pretty good. That is how I believe I received the rhythm that resides deep within my soul. In the segregation cell, I would listen to music through the wall radio, which was tuned to the public radio station. I would listen to the blues every week. There was this sexy voice on Thursdays that played a show from three in the afternoon until six in the evening. The show was called *The Bare Bottom Blues*, and the DJ with the sexy voice called herself Tammy.

I would listen to KZUM all the time and get my dose of blues. And on Sunday night, I would get to jam to the Grateful Dead Hour. I wrote Tammy and requested some Johnny Winter. One of my favorite songs by him is called "Still Alive and Well." Tammy would play it and give me a shout-out every week. We wrote back and forth periodically. She sent me a postcard of the Easy Rider scene, where Captain America and Billy the Kid were going down the highway on their Harley pan heads. I still smile when I think of Jack Nicholson on the back of that motorcycle, wearing a football helmet. Tammy helped me feel that I was not alone, and that is something that I will never forget. *It was hard to keep my love for life alive. I kept my sanity by listening to the blues and letting the music soothe my soul.*

What Is a Normal Day?

There is no such thing as a normal day in prison. Any day can turn into a life-or-death situation. One day I went to the Legal Library. It was about a block and a half from the Control Unit. This is hard when you are walking that far in leg restraints. I was there with the same guy that used to beat on my cell wall when I first entered the Control Unit. Good ole Fat Chuck. While in the library, Fat Chuck tried to get mouthy with a guard and ended up being taken down with force. Then he was escorted back to the Control Unit. Upon arriving back at the Control Unit, Fat Chuck asked me to be his witness against the staff. He thought they used excessive force on him. I laughed at him as I gave him my uncensored opinion of what I thought about him. This led to him telling one of the black gang leaders that he was friends with that they needed to jump that Peckerwood ass cracker (meaning me). This was to take place the next day while we were outside on our recreation hour.

The next day, I put on my boots, then I put rune binds on my hands and feet to invoke strength. In the Asatru lore, the runes are magical. You could combine them to bring forth whatever energy you needed. I proceeded to the recreation yard. There were five men on one yard and five on the other. One man was on the mini-yard. That was how the staff separated the three yards. I was with Fat Chuck and PK; we were on the second yard. I headed straight for Fat Chuck. The leader of the black gang, Big B, asked me if I would squash the beef I had with Fat Chuck. I told him that if he could keep his friend's mouth shut, I would let it go. We agreed to squash it. As soon as I walked away, Fat Chuck started to dance around.

He was shadow boxing and yelled, "I told you that honkey didn't want any of this! That cracker bowed down!"

As I was walking with PK, I stopped dead in my tracks. I turned around and walked straight up to Fat Chuck. He saw the look in my eyes and upon my face. His eyes got real big. Then he sat down thinking I wouldn't do anything to him.

I said, "That isn't going to help you."

I reared back with my leg, and I kicked him square in the mouth. I watched him spit out a mouthful of teeth. I jumped on top of him and started hitting him with a lot of left and right hooks. I put him in a headlock. I tried to get my thumb into his eye socket. I tried to kill him. I heard a long time ago that if you can get your finger in a man's eye socket, you can penetrate his brain with your finger. I tried to take out Fat Chuck this way. As I was trying to penetrate his brain, I heard a gunshot, followed by someone yelling, "I'm shot!"

A guard in the gun tower shot a round into the ground with the intent to have it ricochet into me but missed. I had Fat Chuck up against the fence line, and the guard in the tower didn't have a direct bead on me. The bullet hit another inmate in the buttocks. This man lay on the ground screaming. I got up from Fat Chuck, put my hands in the air, and backed away.

The Control Unit staff was at the gate giving me a direct order to walk into the Control Unit and lock down. I complied with the order and walked into the building. I was strip-searched and went to A-gallery and into my cell. I was never charged with a felony for messing Fat Chuck up, but I did lose a year good time. I thought, hell, it was worth it. I had a good time doing it. I didn't care about anything.

As the days passed by, the unit staff would ask me if I wanted my one-hour recreation time. I would say yes. These yards were separated by a tall fence that had barbed wire and razor wire entwined on top. This ensured that there would be no crawling up the fence and over the top. I walked out of the building and saw that there were five black inmates on the first yard, four on the second yard, and one on the little yard. This meant that I would be the fifth man on the second yard and the only white inmate on the rec yard. I knew the unit staff were trying to have me jumped. Hell, I just tried to kill one of their snitches.

The leader of one of the black gangs, who was protecting Fat Chuck, would have one of his guys try to jump me. Not one of them had the testicular fortitude to try. It wasn't that I was this badass boxer or grappler; I was unpredictable. I did have the reputation of not caring about life—mine, theirs, Fat Chuck's or anyone else's. One day, I was getting ready to jog, and I saw the leader pull one of his guys to the side. He spoke to him through the fence. He was on one side of the fence, and his dude and I were on the other side. As I sat there stretching, his guy came up to me and said, "Hey, Big T, can I jog with you?"

I said to him, "Sure you can, as long as you stay in front of me." What he did not know was that as he bent over to ask me that question, I had a shank in my hand. I was getting ready to bury it in his neck if he made a wrong move. When his leader saw him cower down and coward up, the whole gang ridiculed him. They tore into him verbally. I did not see any punishment for violating an order to take me out. This told me they were on some bullcrap to begin with. I had a reputation for trying to kill a guard and Fat Chuck. I knew that they did not want any problems.

I did not have any problems after that. I started to mellow out. I would spend a lot of time working on my drawing skills. I ended up going eight years without a misconduct report. I was really proud of that.

A Real Friend

I was informed that my oldest son, Joe, had gotten into some trouble. It seemed that no one could handle him. I thank my mother and sisters for trying. Joe was sent to the Omaha Home for Boys. He did really well there. He ended up getting close to a couple that worked there. They eventually took him in as a foster child. Bill and his then wife were very kind and good-hearted people. Joe wanted to come up to the prison to visit me. Bill received permission to bring him up to the prison for a visit. Bill and I hit it off right away; we became good friends. We developed a friendship that lasted for almost twenty years now and counting.

Bill's then wife was a devout Christian and had a Bible sent to me. Bill said to me, "God has a plan for you." I was a practicing heathen and did not take much stock into what was being said. Roger, the man living in the cell next to me, was a Christian. He was struggling in his beliefs, and I am the type of man that leaves no brother behind. Roger was on some heavy medication, and he would get mad. He used to throw his Bible out of his cell and onto the tier from time to time. I took it upon myself to study the Bible with him. I always believed that I should know my enemy. At that time in my life, I considered Christians as my enemy. One thing that I have never forgotten was the one sentence that was said to me: "God has a plan for you."

I continued to draw using pens and ink. Bill created an avenue for me so I could continue to make a difference in people's lives. I would draw these beautiful dragons on envelopes. I would also draw all sorts of stuff, but the artwork was mostly dark in nature. The youngsters who resided at the home would walk into Bill's office and look up at the big basketball backboard that hung behind his desk. The kids would ask him who drew this or who drew that. It gave Bill an opportunity to tell the kids about making bad choices in life. He would also explain to them about the consequences of those choices. I had a few kids that wanted a drawing. Bill told them they had to ask me, which meant they would have to seek permission from their house parents. Then Bill would send me the letter. I would tell them a little about my story, send them a drawing, and hope they would never end up in prison.

What I didn't realize until recently was that was the beginning of helping others. At that time, I was still in active addiction and trying to cope with living in solitary year after year.

As the years rolled on by, I concentrated on my drawing skills and also my communication skills with my family. I had cut off a lot of communication with my family. I believed that I caused them too much pain and I was an embarrassment to them. So after about seven years, I began to open up more dialogue. I am the son who is very close to his mother. I could never figure out why I always hurt her with my actions.

I heard somewhere that we hurt the ones we love the most. Hurting Mom was no different. All my life I have hurt her with my bad choices. I tried to build a relationship with her. What I did not know at the time was the person you are trying to make amends to has the choice to put the deposit in the trust account. I had overdrawn my trust account, and it was bankrupt. It took me years to build the trust back up. All my relationships today are better than they have ever been.

In segregation or in life for that matter, a man that is operating from a selfish center only knows one thing, and that is manipulation. I would whine, snivel, and play on people's sympathy. I would also use the occasional guilt trip to get some money. When I think back over all the years, I can see the pattern of manipulation develop in my life. Manipulation had become a way of life. When I finally became accountable for my actions and responsible for all my decisions, the manipulation stopped.

I kept a loose relationship with Juki and my children. I was never there for them, but I tried to be a dad from prison. This was not good. What could I teach them? I did teach my sons how to be crooks and dope dealers. I had a hard time watching Juki jump from man to man and take my kids along for the ride. I did call them from time to time and write them letters now and then, but this was not until later in my segregation years when I had calmed down and wasn't so violent.

I was allowed two phone calls a week while I was in segregation. I would use one call to talk to my mom. With the other, I would try to call my kids. Most of the time, when I wanted to talk to my kids, it would all depend if Juki answered the phone. When Bill came into my life, I would call him and his wife every couple of weeks. Bill taught me the meaning of what a real friend is. Almost twenty years has passed since Bill and I became friends.

I did not like using the phone in segregation because of the noise from the other inmates. There was an open bullpen that you would have to sit in to use the phone. It meant that every noise that came from the cells would echo into the area. There was banging on the steel doors and banging on the cell walls. The worst was the yelling from one gallery to the other. The respect factor was very low in the segregation unit. I listened to guys yell back and forth, playing chess at 3:00 a.m. Every time I used the phone, I covered one ear with my hand and talked with the other hand.

One thing that is engraved in my memory of Thanksgiving every year. I would always have some tobacco and a little weed. I would eat the turkey dinner and smoke a joint then a cigarette. About noon, I would put on the headphones and listen to Arlo Guthrie Jr. sing "Alice's Restaurant." It seemed that no Thanksgiving Day ever went by that I didn't listen to "Alice's Restaurant." It reminded me of a little piece of my teenage years and into my early twenties. I would go to my grandmother's house, and I would stay in the car a few minutes longer to hear Arlo sing that ballad. I'm not sure if it was the tradition or the fond memories of a time past. Back then, there was a piece of stability in my life; and I yearned for it.

Who Put Out a Hit on Me?

I've seen some real good beatdowns in segregation over disrespect. When a man had enough of it, he would go ballistic and unload verbally on the other guy. This would usually lead to a fight on the rec yard. Some of the men were real creative. One guy waited in the shower until the guard thought he had locked back down in his cell. The man would be all hunkered down, waiting for the guard to open up his neighbor's cell door. This was the neighbor he had words with for three days in a row. The neighbor had been yelling chess numbers out the side of his cell door every night. I witnessed an ugly beating that day. I can't say that I didn't enjoy it. We all took satisfaction when the disrespectful fella got what we thought he deserved.

The disrespect factor is huge in segregation. It seems that when guys get behind a locked door, they will let anything fly out of their mouth. I would call them cell warriors. Most of them were only tough behind a locked cell door. When you are doing time with men who lack respect, it plays a huge game on your psyche.

There were times when the verbiage was so bad and extensive that it would cause a man to go berserk. I've seen men climb razor wire to get to another man because he trash-talked his family for days. This never ended well for the man that lost his cool. He would end up getting all cut up on the wire, or he would try to crawl under the fence that separated him from the man he was trying to put hands on. The result would be him getting stomped before he could get up. *Segregation time was a mental game that many lost at but that everyone had to play.*

I heard my name being thrown about in a conversation between two individuals who were arguing. I heard something about someone put a hit out on me. My ears perked up right away. In segregation, all you hear is loud yelling and talking. You try not to pay any attention to it or it will drive you nuts. When you hear your name being thrown around, you pay attention to it.

I cornered one of the men in the yard the next day, and he confessed to me that a few years prior, his buddy Tessie tried to get him to take me out of the game. He said that I hated Mexicans and would try to hurt him. Of course, this was a lie. A few of his friends told him that I was a solid convict. Even though I was a racist, I did not go around hurting people without a reason. I told him that his bro RH and Lil Temple had told me a few years ago to watch my back around Flowboy and Tessie. Now it all made sense to me. I cornered Tessie, and he swore up and down that he did not put a hit out on me, but I already knew the truth. Tessie was a snake and had a rat jacket on him. I had done too much time and saw him in action for years, so nothing that came out of his mouth was believable. I told him that as long as he was alive and in the same prison as I was, he would have to pay. I made him give me half of everything he got his hands on—dope, money, tobacco, it didn't matter. I got half of it. This went on even when he got out of the seg unit. He didn't last long on the yard in general population. This man could not stay out of trouble or mind his own business, which brought him a lot of unnecessary heartache.

When he finally emerged from the segregation unit this last time, which was in 2014, I had already changed my life. I walked up to him and told him that he owed me nothing. I explained to him why I did what I did to him. I told him how I changed my life, and I only wanted good things for him. He went on to tell me all he wanted to do was stay high and he would stay out of my way.

As the years rolled on in the segregation unit, I realized that consistency was the best cure for boredom. I worked out every day except on the weekends. I got into jogging on the tiny yard during my one hour of recreation time. I found a book about yoga that was on the book cart. I started doing yoga every day. I became really good doing the poses. I could stand on my head for some time. I loved stretching, and my body was in great shape.

The staff that worked in the unit still took the occasional shot at me. One day, I was standing on my head meditating. I heard the hatch in the cell door open. I thought it was mail call, but nothing hit the floor. I heard a big slam. I automatically jerked my head to see what had happened, but I already knew. The guard had slammed the steel hatch. He stood there looking in the little window, laughing. I was pissed. My standing-on-my-head days were over. I pulled a neck muscle when I twisted my head. It would take years to heal.

6

Can I Get a Hug?

I went to my unit manager and asked him to support me for a promotion from intensive management to administrative segregation. He laughed and told me that he would get ridiculed and possibly fired for even suggesting it. He was serious about the ridiculed part. I was not a liked inmate, and I knew it would be a longshot to get any support for a downgrade in custody level. It was 2001, and I had been without a misconduct report for seven or eight years. I still couldn't get a break.

I waited six months and approached the unit manager again. This time, he said he would support me no matter how much ridicule he would receive over it. I couldn't believe my eyes when I received the classification paper. The administration approved the reduction in my custody level. I was now on A/C (administrative confinement). This meant I could receive contact visits and be able to touch another person. I was about to get a hug, maybe even a kiss.

I contacted Bill, and he came down to visit me on a Saturday morning. I was cuffed up and escorted across the yard to turnkey. This was where the segregation visits were held. The restraints were removed, and I was strip-searched before I could enter the visiting room. There are things in prison that you have to condition yourself to. Being strip-searched all the time is one of them. Getting naked in front of other people does not bother me at all. I am numb to it. I walked into the visiting room and saw Bill sitting there waiting for me. I walked up to him and gave him a big hug. My bro knew that it was the first contact I had with anyone in years.

When I sat down, I knew that I had to get used to the crowds of people that were in the room, which was a very hard thing to do and still is to this day. I think that all the years I spent being alone in segregation took its toll on me. I am overwhelmed when I am in a crowd of people. I sat there and felt very uncomfortable. I do not like noise. The thing about a prison visiting room is it's very noisy. I had a great visit with Bill. I tried to assure him I was okay. I knew that he was aware that I was not comfortable. It was hard being around a lot of people at one time.

As the weeks rolled on by, I would get more comfortable in the room. I did find a trick that worked. I was getting Juki to bring my kids up to see me, and I would have her show up late. This allowed us to be placed in a small room by ourselves.

I eventually had her coming up by herself so I could mess around. I had a guard in my pocket. He was getting paid to bring me in tobacco. He was getting paid from my bro to carry a package into the segregation unit. Every few weeks, I was getting contraband.

I would have the same guard put Juki in the back classroom, which was being used as a spare visiting room. He would give us about ten minutes to mess around. It had been over a decade since I had touched a woman or received a kiss. I learned that I lost all that loving feeling. Juki was just an object.

I was having my oldest son bring me in packages through the visiting room. One thing that I did not realize at the time was how I had been so self-centered. I did not care who I was putting in harm's way. I also did not realize that I was being a negative influence in his life. I was teaching him how to break the law. I was a bad father. *I couldn't and shouldn't even call myself a father. I do not deserve that title.* What I did not know at the time was I was setting my son up for failure. He would eventually get arrested for transporting methamphetamines across state lines. He received a seven-year sentence and served it in the federal prison system.

I was having my knee scoped out; it was full of torn cartilage. I believe when the guard had my knee bent backward, he damaged it. Running in circles in the small yard did not help either. My health was starting to deteriorate. I thought it was from all the years spent in segregation.

I was also diagnosed with hepatitis C. I had a liver biopsy done. It showed I had cirrhosis (stage 4). *I was given five years to live.* I could extend my life if I took the treatment. The liver specialist set me up for the treatment, which would be like having chemo. The treatment would consist of a weekly shot of interferon and daily doses of ribavirin for six months. Before I could start the treatment, I was transferred to the segregation unit in the new maximum security prison that was just built in Tecumseh, Nebraska.

There's a Barnyard in Hell with a Countryside View

In October 2002, a new chapter began. My new home reminded me of my heart—empty and cold. I went through the strip searches and answered questions that were the same in any facility upon entering. Do you have any enemies? Do you need medical attention? Do you feel like hurting yourself? I do not remember saying no so many times in one sitting. This took a few hours. I couldn't wait to go to the cell and see where I would reside for the next who knows how long.

I was escorted to a cell on F block. As I entered the gallery, I could smell the urine and feces. I remember that smell from somewhere. Oh yeah, the zoo. It was a "straight in your face" barnyard aroma. All I heard, as I walked down the gallery, was a few guys who were behind their cell doors talking in the vents. My name was mentioned, and the passing of the messages began through the vents. One of these men knew who I was. Talking through the vents was a way to pass messages from the upper tier to the lower tier and from one end of the wing to the other. I soon realized I was on a wing full of crazies.

Part of the problem of doing time in a segregation unit is that it is full of mentally challenged men. When the state decided to close down a few of the mental wards, all the state's mentally challenged had nowhere to go. The police would arrest them, and they would go to prison. The only way they could survive in prison was to go to segregation. It is a sad thing, but all prisons have a high population of mentally challenged people in their segregation units.

Within a few days, I was settling into my new cell. The view was great. I had a big tall window that overlooked the countryside. The yard that I would exercise in was no bigger than the cell I lived in. The sun did not reach into it; it was under an eave and had a heavy gage steel fence on the only open side. Three sides cement walls and one side steel fence. I could have conversations with men that were in other wings. There were two yards next to each other and on top of each other. Four men at one time could converse with each other.

I couldn't get over the disrespect that the guards had for all the inmates that were housed in segregation. I discovered why the cellblock smelled like a barnyard. It seemed that the not-right-in-the-head inmates would get treated badly, and to retaliate, they would throw feces on the guards. A lot of men would solve their arguments by tossing urine and feces in their enemy's cell. I scratched my head on that one. I never did get used to living next to men like that. I heard them scream at all hours of the night and day. They would also bang on the cell doors at all hours and flood the cellblock with water. As I look back, I am amazed that I kept my sanity through the thirteen years of chaos.

In my opinion, the visits were terrible. I would be locked in a small room with full restraints. The guard would remove one cuff so I could hold a phone. Your visitor would be in a room that was in another part of the prison. They would have to talk to you through a TV monitor. Segregation visits were not good. *No physical touching was permitted; it was total isolation.* I missed the contact visits that I had back at the penitentiary.

My case manager was a former sergeant at the penitentiary and a member of the good old-boy society. The first thing he did was delete all the positive things that I had accomplished in the past several years. He told me that I had to start all over. My argument with him was "If you delete the good, then you should also delete the bad. Now let me out of this hellhole." His response was more or less in the words of "If you do not like it, then sue me." He would eventually end up being part of the lawsuit that I filed to get out of segregation. All I knew was I was up against a lot of opposition, and the good old boys had long memories.

I was getting shorted on my meals by being served small portions. The guard who ran the yard would trim about fifteen to twenty minutes off my yard time. On shower days, I would be skipped over, and when I would question the staff about it, they would tell me that they asked me and I had refused. I knew that once again, everyone had to take their shot at me. I believed they did this intentionally to feed their egos. Most of the guards were full of fear and lacked testicular fortitude. I did not react when they took their shots at me. My reacting days were over. I numbed myself to all of it. I observed their actions, and I studied them. I knew just how they would react to any given situation. Who really controlled who? Segregation time eventually became entertaining.

One day I was on a visit with Juki. I was standing there in the little room with one hand out of the cuffs. The door opened up, and there stood a captain, the same man that was a sergeant a few years ago at the state pen. This was the same man that had put the boots to me when I was in full restraints. I saw a reflection in the hallway window that started to move. Two guards were standing behind the outer wall of the room I was in. I felt like I was being set up. I had been around a long time. I knew how to deal with the situation—do what they do not expect me to do. I smiled and stuck my hand out. The captain looked surprised, and he shook my hand. We talked a few minutes about my health and how I was adjusting to life at Tecumseh. As soon as our conversation was up, the two guards walked around the door and cuffed me up. They wore a look of disappointment on their faces as they escorted me back to my cell.

I thought about retaliation for a split second. However, I was on a different path in life, but I was not sure what path it was. I just knew I was done being violent. Was I broken? Did the years in segregation mellow me out? I had no clue as to why I was changing. All I know is I was tired, really tired of being kept in a seven-by-nine-foot cell.

In the middle of 2003, I had another six-month segregation review. This time, I had a couple of the good old boys on the board.

One member was friends with the guard that I had assaulted. He sat there and mean-mugged me. I smiled. He began the hearing by telling me that I had hurt his friend and I was lower than an animal. He continued to tell me that I would never get out of segregation as long as he had anything to do with it. I had heard that rhetoric before. I told him that I thought I was entitled to a fair review. He laughed at me. I told him I would get the last laugh when I filed a federal lawsuit pertaining to a fair and impartial review.

I did grievance the review process. For some odd reason, I was given a new review. It consisted of a new set of board members but the same results. Six more months in segregation for being a threat to the safety and security of the institution was their reasoning.

I was moved to a wing that held death row. The administration started an incentive program which was for inmates that were staying out of trouble. It was a wing that was supposed to be quieter. A guy could use a pull-up bar and a dip bar to exercise on that gallery. The gallery had twenty-two cells. Ten cells held death row and twelve were for the incentive guys. I had a friend that was on death row. Living on the same run gave me time to talk with him and see him every day. Another reason I liked living with the guys on the row was I got help putting my lawsuit together. These men knew their way around the court system, and I used their knowledge to learn how to win my suit and get out of the hole. In the fall of 2003, I filed a suit in the federal courts. I knew that thirteen years in segregation was overkill, and my Eighth and Fourteenth Amendment rights were being violated.

I was in contact with the states ombudsman's office, seeking help with medical issues concerning my messed-up knee and the use of segregation as punishment. The ombudsman that had my case was a man named James. James is a good person who assisted me with getting out of segregation. He worked hard and for quite a bit of time to get the director to let me out. I am grateful to him to this day. There are people like James that do care and try to make a wrong right.

Roll Up! You're Going to General Population

On January 6, 2004, I was standing in my cell exercising when the hatch in my cell door opened and a guard tossed three large garbage bags into my cell. He told me to pack up because I was being released from the segregation unit and going to general population. I laughed at him and said, "Okay! I will get right on that." He walked away and I thought, *What a piece of crap, playing head games with me.* For the past thirteen years, they had been playing one head game or another.

Ten minutes later, the guard was back at my cell door and said, "Fleming, I'm serious. You're being released from segregation, so hurry up. I have to take you to the deputy warden's office in ten minutes."

I stood there in my cell, stunned and confused. After spending thirteen years in segregation, I was finally getting out. I did not know what to put in the bag first. My friend in the cell next to me yelled, "Just throw it all in the bag, brother, and worry about separating it later! You're getting out!"

I did not know what to think or how to act. *Being locked up in a seven-by-nine-foot cell was my life. Isolation was my world.* All of that was about to change in ten minutes. The guard came with a cart. I put all my belongings on it, and I walked out of the cell. When the cell door shut, I got into the position to allow the guard to put the restraints on me. The guard said, "You won't be getting cuffed up. You are released. Just follow me. We are going to the deputy warden's office."

That was a long walk. When I got to the deputy warden's office, he was sitting there with a look on his face that told me he wasn't happy about this release. Then he told me he was releasing me to general population and that I would be getting a clean slate and a fresh start. He told me to not blow it and wished me luck. Now I am no dummy and knew that a clean slate will never happen, especially within the good old boy system where they never forgive nor forget. I knew something was not right when he wished me luck. This was the same man that used to dish out grief to me by the bucketful when he was a sergeant at the state penitentiary.

It was a very cold day when I walked out of the deputy warden's office. I had to push my property in a cart to Housing Unit One. The temperature was zero outside, and the wind was blowing hard. I always said it would be a cold day in hell when I would get out of the segregation unit. Here it was, a cold day. Tecumseh State Correctional Institution was no different than the other prisons in the state. They are all a hell.

When I walked into the housing unit, I saw Nose standing there talking with Crow. These were two of my closest bros. They came up and gave me a hug. They could not believe that I had gotten out of the bucket. I went to the cell that I was assigned to and tossed all my property onto the cell floor. I then walked into the dayroom where all the fellas were. They lined up to give me handshakes. They also tried to give me this new thing, which was a fancy dap with a hug. I was not having any of that crap. I did not hug anyone that wasn't a good bro. The problem I saw with this new breed of inmate was that they were too free with their trust and brotherly affection.

I did notice that some men were giving respect to those that did not earn it. This made it hard for guys like me. I did not trust anyone who wasn't put between a rock and a hard place. If a man was put in the hole, held his mud, which simply means he kept his mouth shut, and he carried his own weight, only then could he be trusted. I saw men let other men get too close to them. The men that they allowed near them were known snitches. When an old convict would tell them that they were hanging with a rat, they would say, "I thought that dude was cool. He always has good pot." I thought it was a shame for a man to set his respect levels on the basis of whether a man had good weed or not.

I saw my good friend Dawg sitting at a table writing his book. He spotted me and got up. We shook hands then talked for a few minutes. Dawg explained to me what his book was about. He asked me if I wrote a book yet. I told him that I have nothing to say that anyone would be interested in. My bro encouraged me over the years to write. Dawg and I have a plan to hook up and build a shovelhead if I ever made it out of prison alive. Dawg is a Native American and lives on the Winnebago Reservation. He loves to write and also builds motorcycles. I have met a lot of good people over the years.

It did not take long for me to get around and see all the fellas. I was known as Big T, the dude who did thirteen years in the bucket or one of the dudes from the trash truck escape. I was also known as Tyrok, one of the elders who started Asatru in the Nebraska prison system. One thing that I always made sure of was that I had a good rapport with all the heads of the other races and the leaders of the various gangs. Respect is something that you have to give before you can receive. That is the old-school rules. I was a man that was, and still am, respected in many circles.

As the weeks rolled on by, I would meet the other men that my bros had checked out as good men. I had the weed connection, and I met the tobacco connection. I was in, and I did not waste any time getting into the mix. The one drawback about being in the mix was the prison snitches were always watching.

Men would tell on me for anything and embellish on it. Time after time, I was hauled up to the captain's office and questioned about the numerous snitch kites that they had received about me. My cell was routinely searched. At one point, I was under scrutiny for timing the perimeter vehicle, which amounted to nothing but me standing on the track that ran around the ballfield. I was watching a couple of pheasants that were walking in the cornfield that surrounded the prison. I would just laugh at the captain and tell him the truth, but sometimes they didn't want to hear the truth.

I did find out that the administration had a couple of well-known informants watch my every move. They were reporting on everything that I did throughout the day, and especially who I was talking with. I thought that the information that I was given sounded crazy. I knew it had to be true because it came from an officer. I loved it when a certain correctional officer would hip me to what was going on at their roll call. I still do not know why, but I enjoyed the information. I suspected that he was a racist and a sympathizer to my way of life.

I did have a captain that knew me from the time he was an officer of the lowest rank back at the state pen. He told me that he knew the snitch kites were frivolous, but he still had to investigate me. I told him that all I wanted was a fair shake and a full investigation before he threw me back in the bucket. Over the years, he kept his word, and I did not get thrown back in the segregation unit until he didn't have a choice.

I got together with some like-minded folks that were Asatru. The first thing they wanted me to do was join their kindred. I had to check these guys out, and I really liked a couple of them and heard good things about them. I felt that the group they had was okay, and I would see where it would go. Like a lot of things in prison, it takes time for the truth to emerge. I ran a poker table and had some of the fellas involved. I was also hustling dope and tobacco. I found out one self-proclaimed leader was stealing the money we were making. He ended up completing his sentence from the segregation unit. I stayed away from the Asatru land and all kindred activities for quite some time. I just did not like the breed of people. I would have no part of their kindred.

I did not like hypocrisy. As I watched all the men around me, I started to fade into the background a bit. I still had my reputation and my racist values. I started to gather some of the strong men whom I thought had the same values and racial beliefs as I had. A few of these men had some ghosts in their closets. I ended up overlooking some of their flaws, only because I saw that they had some strong areas that I could use in the future. It would be a bad decision in the end.

I Refuse to Die in Prison

In 2005, I became sick and needed my gallbladder removed. I had been hurting real bad in my stomach area. I went up to medical to see what was up. After some tests, I was told that my gallbladder needed to be taken out. It seemed that between the hep C and the dope, I had developed a huge gallstone. I was taken down to the little county hospital and had the surgery.

I started to swell up a few days after the operation, and I didn't know what was going on. I was sitting in a chair in the visiting room visiting with my friend Bill when I started to leak fluid out of the incision sites. Bill told me that I needed to take my ass to medical right away.

I left the visiting room in pain. I informed my unit staff. They called the medical staff. I was told to lie down and all would be okay. I did lie down, and in the middle of the night, I woke up and found myself lying in a puddle of yellowish fluid. And I mean a puddle. I was soaked. I called out to the guard that was walking around doing his hourly cell checks, and I told him that I needed help. I was taken to the infirmary and put in a room. I asked the night nurse for some bedding, and she handed me a bag to put my clothes in. She then told me in a sarcastic tone that I could change my own soiled dressings. Yep! I had found another hater. It seemed that there were a few haters in the system who thought I should die for what I had done in 1991.

The next day, the doctor walked in and told me that I was not going to make it. My liver was shutting down, and it couldn't handle the operation I had gone through. He told me that he was going to contact my family. I told him that there was no way in hell. I would not die in a prison hospital. (This was my biggest fear, dying in a prison hospital.). He looked at me with a sneer upon his face. By this time I had put on forty pounds of fluid. I was swelled up real good, and my scrotum was the size of a head of lettuce. My veins quit processing the fluid normally and were pushing the fluid into my body cavity, causing the swelling. I was a mess and really pondered if this might be it, but I just couldn't wrap my mind around dying.

A nurse finally found a vein and started pushing meds in me to try to take some of the fluid out of me. The doctor then took a sulfur stick and started to burn the incisions closed. He was burning me in the places that I was leaking fluid from. I was in pain and thought, *What a sadistic bastard, burning me without numbing the area first.* Can you imagine how sensitive the skin is from all the swelling? Then to be burned closed in three incision sites. The doctor eventually was terminated a few years later for unrelated misconduct violations.

I lay up in that cold infirmary room for a few weeks, and my will to live got me through it. I was released back into general population and was given a pair of boxer/briefs to wear so I could have some support for my scrotum. I had a hard time walking for a few weeks, but the swelling eventually subsided.

I started to work out and do cardio. I would walk every day, and it took a few months before I was halfway healthy again. The physician's assistant, who was a good person and really tried to help people, told me that she thought I was healthy enough to try the hep C treatment again. Only this time, she would monitor the blood work and would adjust the doses as needed so I could get through the six-month treatment. This would be three doses of ribavirin daily and a weekly shot of interferon. This was equivalent to chemotherapy. My hair started to fall out, and I felt like I had the flu every day. This was a long six months, but I made it and it was successful. I am in remission and have been for over a decade. To this day, my liver functions are normal.

There were two things that I used as comforters. I taught myself how to play the bass guitar. I also taught myself how to paint. I love my music. I can rock out all night long. *I firmly believe that music soothes the soul.* I was lucky enough to hook up with a couple of guys and form a band that played classic rock. We played in the prison's gym four times. I had a blast every time I was in front of my peers. It was cool to make music and see your friends having a good time, nodding in rhythm with the beat.

I taught myself to paint with pastels. I also learned to mix media. I eventually mastered watercolor. Bill and his former wife had some friends in Texas that they wanted to give a gift to. They asked me to paint a picture of their friend's dogs. I was eager to paint four dogs sitting on a couch. I loved the way the painting turned out. The men that I painted it for loved it too. It wasn't long after I had given the painting to Bill so he could deliver to Texas that I received a thank-you letter with a sizable money order from the dog's owners. This allowed me to purchase better supplies to paint with. I would soon be the guy that painted dog portraits in pastel.

7

Forgiveness

The year 2006 was a year that would change my life forever. I was called to the unit manager's office, and there sat a counselor who happened to be a mediator for the Victim/Offender Dialogue Program (also known as VOD). She asked me if I would participate in the VOD, and I asked why. She proceeded to tell me that the guard that I had hurt wanted some answers as to why he was so severely assaulted. I told the lady that all that information was in the court documents, and all the court documents were accessible to the public. Then she told me that Mr. F wanted to know if he was targeted because he walked funny. I told her to give me a few days to think about it.

The following week, I was called back into her office, and I said, "As a man, I respect all men who have the testicular fortitude to face their fears." I told her that I did have some worries that Mr. F wanted to get some kind of payback or try to take a swing at me, maybe even wanted to spit on me. I was not sure the real reason for it. I was assured that this VOD was on the up-and-up. I, with my big ego, also thought that if the man I had harmed wanted to meet me face-to-face, he had some guts. I was up for the encounter. What did I have to lose anyway? I was dying and only had a short time to live. I was troubled a little about how Mr. F thought that he was hurt bad because he walked funny.

Prepping for the meeting took a few months. The mediators needed to be sure that the victim and the offender were mentally and emotionally stable for the meeting. I spent a lot of time wondering what my peers would think. I struggled with telling anyone for a long time it was my business and no one else's. Over the weeks preceding the meeting, I wondered if I was doing the right thing. I knew deep down in my gut something was about to change, but I just did not know the what or to what degree. There were questions that were asked and a few questions that I expected would be asked during the meeting. I was ready.

The meeting was in the visiting room, and it was on a non-visiting day, so there was no traffic in the visiting room. I walked into the room. It had two long tables with four chairs around them. I was directed to sit there by my mediator. Then the other mediator walked in and introduced herself. I recognized her. She was once my probation officer years ago. How ironic, I thought. She made sure that I was ready, and then she said that we could start the meeting.

Mr. F walked into the room. I had been instructed to just sit there and wait for him to start the dialogue, and then answer him when he asked me a question. The first thing Mr. F did was lean across the table and extended his hand. We shook hands, and he thanked me for meeting with him. I was a little shocked, because I did not expect that to happen. One thing it did do was put me at ease. Mr. F started talking about that day, August 31, 1991. Wow, I didn't realize that fifteen years had passed by.

Mr. F asked me what my part was in the escape attempt. He said he had read all the reports and also heard the accounts of that day from other people. He wanted to know my reasoning for what had happened. I explained what had happened from the time I woke up that day. I also explained to him how I tried to get the keys from his belt. He wanted to know not only why I had stabbed him but also why PK had set him on fire. This was hard for me to talk about, but I told him the reasons. It was not because he walked funny. I thought to myself that it must have been very mind-blowing for a man to go through life thinking that he was assaulted because he walked funny. This was another reason I had wanted to participate in the VOD. I wanted to clear that up for him. He told me that I was the only one that had agreed to meet with him.

We talked about a lot of things that day. The meeting lasted almost three hours. The things that hit me the most was when Mr.

F explained to me how my actions of August 31 had affected him physically, mentally, emotionally, and spiritually. He explained to me how his children had handled what had happened to him and what they went through. He told me what my actions did to his marriage and what it did to his coworkers. He went into detail about how my actions affected his family and friends. He talked about the pain and the years of torment he went through. Healing from the burns took years. Then he told me about how he helped a little child who was in the burn center with him. The young child was going through the same things he was going through. I recognized that it takes courage and a big heart to be able to do something that powerful. Then Mr. F asked me how my actions of that day affected me and my family. He asked me how I was treated during those thirteen years in segregation. It surprised me that he would take great interest in how I was treated. I was impacted greatly by the question about my family and the way that my actions had affected them. These were things that I never thought about before, on any level.

Mr. F had given me a lot to think about that day, and it would change my life forever. As the meeting was about over, Mr. F asked me if he could write a letter of support to the parole board for me. I told him that it was not necessary because I was given only five years to live. I would not make it to see a parole date. My earliest eligibility was May 2017. Then Mr. F walked up to me and shook my hand, and he put his other hand on my shoulder. He looked me in the eyes and thanked me for meeting with him. He said that he forgives me for everything that I did on August 31, 1991. Both of us stood there looking at each other with tears in our eyes. He smiled at me and walked out of the room.

I sat there for a few minutes, stunned. I did not deserve that man's forgiveness, or at least that's what I thought at that time. Forgiveness was the foundation that would change my life forever. It was a few years before the importance of that meeting sunk into my thick head. *Today, I fully understand what had taken place.*

I went back to the housing unit that day and locked myself in my cell. I lay down on my bunk and smiled. It was as if a big weight was removed from my shoulders. I felt lighter. I thought that if I died right now, that very moment, I would be okay. Mr. F had put his hand on my shoulder while he looked me in the eyes, and he forgave me. What I would soon realize was that just because Mr. F had forgiven me did not mean that any of the other guards or the prison officials would ever forgive me. Nor would they ever forget what I did. Every day in prison was a constant reminder of what I had done and who I was.

I kept that meeting to myself for a long time. I knew what the social mirror was like. I still had to keep my reputation intact. Even though I did not do anything wrong meeting with Mr. F, there is still a code of conduct within the prison system. The convict code says you do not talk to staff. I did not tell Mr. F anything that was not already known. I was proud of myself for helping Mr. F find some closure as to what had happened to him that awful day fifteen years prior.

As the months passed by, I was still heavy into my addictions. I would get my weekly supply of tobacco and weed. Then I would be at the poker tables every day, all day, making money. My health was poor, and I knew I was dying slowly. I still didn't care. My mental attitude was that I would go out my way to get high. I was relieved that I had helped Mr. F. Now I just wanted to stay high until I died.

I lost the urge to stick a needle in my arm. I didn't want to shoot dope anymore. This confused me. I was still smoking pot and cigarettes, and I would have the occasional tumbler of hooch. That was soon to change. On my birthday, December 31, 2007, I was in my cell with a pouch of tobacco and a stick of weed. I was drinking hooch (prison beer). I had two full tumblers on the desk. I was standing on the toilet so I could blow the smoke from the cigarette and weed into the vent. I knew that the guard wouldn't smell it. I used to tape off the output vent. This allowed all the smoke to flow into the intake vent. This prison trick prevented anyone that was outside the cell from smelling anything. I stood there looking at the joint that I just had lit and the cigarette that I was smoking. I felt something deep down inside, and I knew I was done. All the smoking, drinking, and getting high had taken its toll on me. I did not want to do any of it anymore. I had lost my appetite to get high. I stopped right then and there.

Respect/Disrespect

I was the Elder Gothi of the Asatru kindred, and I held a lot of the rituals on the Ve. A Ve is plot of land that is for holding religious practices. The Native Americans and the Wiccans have a little plot of land also that is adjacent to the Asatru land. When I say land, I am talking about a plot that is around fifteen by twenty-five feet long. As I held these rituals, it seemed something was amiss. Something had changed in me. I was a Gothi, and I could not step down. We had incorporated a lot of white supremacy propaganda into the lessons we were teaching. It was a requirement to read white power books that we had smuggled into the institution, along with some white power music from underground skinhead bands. We were beating the Aryan drum.

The Native Americans were having their yearly freedom run. It was held every year on the quarter of a mile track that ran around the softball field. They invited us to participate, and we accepted. On that particular Saturday morning, we all met at the peckerwood pavilion. This was an area that we put claim to. We had our poker tables there, and it was also a meeting place for all the like-minded folk. We walked in unison to the ballfield. There were about fifteen of us that wanted to participate. We had pledged to the Natives that we would run three miles. As soon as we hit the ballfield, all heads turned toward us. The guards looked nervous and thought we were there to kick up some dust. I took the lead and had two rows behind me. Each row had seven men in it. As soon as we were finished jogging the three miles, the Native that was holding the sacred staff, which was wrapped in buffalo hide, handed it off to me. This was an honorable gesture. I took the place of honor and ran a few laps, leading everyone that was participating in the run.

To be asked to carry the sacred staff meant that there was a very deep level of respect. This was something that I thought was very deep on many levels. It also meant that we would have peace with the Natives. As soon as we walked off the ballfield, there were about ten guards, including sergeants and captains, at the entrance. They were there waiting for an altercation to break out. We walked past them laughing. I knew we now had heat on us, and it would not end in a good way.

We were holding fighting technique classes in the religious center. The guard would sit outside the door and not have a clue. There were a lot of punching and takedown lessons from a couple of military guys who knew some MMA training. We thought we were untouchable. We made gloves that had gel padding inside of them, and you could get hit without leaving a mark. This went on for a while. We even had classes on taking over an armored car if we ever made it to the streets. What I did not know was, no one was checking up on the guy who was lore keeper. A lore keeper is the man who writes down all the kindred's activities, but only in code. Everyone thought the man knew what he was doing. *Oops!*

The guards were doing a cell search and found the lore book. I was told that so-and-so just got booked, which means sent to segregation. This was early March 2009. The other two Gothis came and got me, and we went to the religious coordinator's office, which is in the religious center where our religious locker is. The one kinsman asked me to talk to the coordinator and see why there was another lock on the locker, preventing us from getting into it. I was told that the captain had it sealed for investigation. When I went in to tell the two kinsmen, I found them trying to break into the bottom of the locker, and one of them looked really nervous. I knew they had something hidden in there, but I did not know what. If I had known ahead of time that it was escape paraphernalia, it would have never been in there to begin with.

Off to the segregation unit I went, this time for escape paraphernalia. I was very pissed and confused. *Who would disrespect me like this? Total betrayal!* To have put any type of escape material in the locker, especially knowing that I have a history for attempting to escape, was very upsetting to me. If anything like that turned up anywhere around me, I could be buried in the hole. I never did receive a misconduct report, but the warden wanted me in segregation. He wanted to keep me there for a *long* time.

Come to find out, one of my kinsmen had been planning to escape. He had not only plans drawn out but also had handwritten letters to his family in case he got killed trying to escape. That saved me from dying in segregation; the brass knew it wasn't me. It was a man that was supposedly under my leadership. I felt really disrespected. From that time on, I knew that I was being used for my reputation. I ended up doing thirteen months in the segregation unit. Before I was let out, I was told that if I went back to the Ve, I would be thrown back in the hole. This was all unofficial. I was told to never pick up a horn again or I would die in segregation. Picking up a horn meant that I was hailing the gods and goddesses, leading the men. I gave my word that I would comply. One thing about doing thirteen months in the hole, it reminded me of the previous thirteen years I had spent in segregation. I was sick to my stomach for a long time.

I did get in good shape while I was in segregation, but I completely tore the ACL in my right knee. I was back on the yard limping around. It got so bad that they gave me an MRI on my knee. I was told that I did not have an ACL and would need to undergo surgery. They would use part of my hamstring to replace it. This would keep me in a leg stint for seven weeks. It took up to almost a year before it was healed.

From the time I was released from segregation in 2010 until the summer of 2012, I kept away from all the Asatru activities. I could not shake some of the guys from hanging with me. These were my brothers, and one of them was like a son to me. It hurt me to back away from the kinsman, but something inside of me was changing. It seemed that it all made sense to me. I did not like who I was anymore. I did not allow more than two people to walk with me, and I would not stand around in crowds. I did not want to ever again return to a segregation unit. I also had a deep hatred toward the two men that had betrayed me during the locker incident.

8

New Beginnings

My friend Bill came down to Tecumseh to visit me, and he brought his new wife, Deb, with him to meet me. I was very impressed with Deb. She has a good head on her shoulders. She even rode her own Harley, which I thought was cool. I was really happy to see Bill smile from the heart. It had been a long time since I had seen him this happy and content. I recognized that he was not in a good place for quite a few years. We used to have in-depth conversations when he would visit me every few weeks. I loved to listen to Bill talk about what was going on in the world. All those years in segregation and being in prison, I felt secluded from the reality of what was transpiring outside the prison walls. I felt blessed to have a friend outside of the prison. We have been friends since that first time he brought my son Joe down to see me, and I believe that was around nineteen or twenty years now.

By the end of 2012, there were a lot of assaults taking place. Someone was putting hits on all the snitches and some of the high-profile child molesters. I had already given up all my power. I was no longer leading the men. I was not in the loop as to what the kindred was involved in. I had my suspicions that all the gangs were cleaning up their messes. At some point, they got together and decided to clean up the yard.

Before I went to the segregation unit in 1991, the yard didn't have all the open snitching that it had when I walked out of the segregation unit in 2004. I saw not only open snitching but also saw high-profile pedophiles walking the yard. Somewhere between 1991 and 2004, the yard had turned in its politics. Back in the day, the snitches and the child molesters were not allowed to walk the yard. That was what the protective custody units were for.

I was talking to the Substance Abuse Unit supervisor about getting into SAU because I wanted to find out why I was an addict. He assisted me in enrolling. I was allowed in, even though I was not required to take it. I no sooner moved into the SAU than the yard went on lockdown. The administration was fed up with all the daily assaults on the yard and in the housing units. All prisons in Nebraska were on some kind of modified lockdown these days, except Omaha Correctional Center.

The first cellmate I had in twenty years was a kid who was doing his first stretch of time. He was very scared. It did not help the situation when everyone told him who I was, what I was in for, and all the segregation time I had done. This kid had to be in his early twenties and was a meth head. For the first month, the kid slept like a fireman, fully clothed and ready to jump in his boots the first time he heard something move. It took me a month to get him to settle down and convinced that I was not a weirdo or a booty bandit (we used to call the rapists in prison booty bandits). Come to find out a few of his friends were messing with him and filling his head with a bunch of untruths. I squashed that right away because I did not need a paranoid kid in my cell.

It took me a while to teach this kid how to do time. I told him not to chew his fingernails and let them fall from his top bunk onto me or my bunk. I had to teach him how the law of gravity worked. Everything that is up will fall down, including all the dirt on his boots. I said, "Do not climb up on the bunk with boots on." I have a no shoes on policy when in the top bunk. I came back to the cell after chow one day, and the day room was open.

Michael, a guy in the next cell over, said to me, "Don't step to the left." I looked down, and there was a puddle of piss by the toilet. I immediately started to scan the dayroom for the kid because I was going to rub his nose in it. Michael spotted the kid before I did and took off to explain to him what he did and to go clean it up. The kid acted as if it was not a big deal. That pissed me off more than him pissing on the floor. It took all I had not to put hands on the kid. This was very humbling for me to practice patience and tolerance. The kid was a good kid. He was a meth head that got caught selling it. Now he had to serve his time.

I was able to move him out of the cell in two months. Every two months there was a graduation, and cells would open up. It gave the men an opportunity to cell with someone they were compatible with. I moved in a guy whose name is Johnny G. He just violated his parole for the third time. Johnny G was a Bible thumper who always left God back in the prison when he paroled. We would have very deep and heated conversations about God and Christianity.

I was also working with a counselor, Dan, who was a pastor, but he couldn't officially talk about God because of the church and state thing. He would ask me to read certain books, and then we would talk about them. He was not my one-on-one counselor. Jennifer was, and she was good. She used to be a guard and knew me. She knew what I was about. Her mother, sister, and her sister's husband also worked for the prison in Tecumseh. One day, during one of our many one-on-one sessions, she told me how I was a part of their dinner conversation.

One day I was at medical, and her mother was taking my vitals when a doctor pulled her out of the room. He was very disrespectful to her, and she was visibly shaken when she walked back into the room. I told her that I had heard the whole conversation. I then told her that if she would like, I would go out and shove all the doctor's teeth down his throat for her. I was a very violent man who did not think about the consequences of my actions. I asked her what year this took place, and she told me around 2005. I smiled because it was before my VOD meeting. I did not even think about the promise I had given the administration, the one where I said I would not harm anyone.

I had been reading these Christian-themed books and higher power books for Dan's class and conversing with Johnny about his religion. I kept thinking about what Bill had told me way back in 1998. He said, "God has a plan for you." This started me on a course to find my true higher power.

I was working with Jennifer on some personal issues about change and that I did not like myself anymore. She asked me why I always fell back on the meeting with Mr. F. I was always talking about forgiveness, but I couldn't forgive myself or others. It seemed to her that my new foundation for change was based on forgiveness. I did not see it at first, and then my eyes were opened. When I talked about myself, I would talk about the VOD, only I did not know when this started. I had been openly talking about the VOD as if I were an advocate.

Forgiveness was the thing that I did not quite understand. When I think about forgiveness, I think about how I was always the guy that said, "I'm sorry," but then repeated the mistake. I would also forgive one of the fellas but still have animosity toward him. This forgiveness that I had just received was something that felt totally different. It was as if I was free, in an odd sort of way. Things in my life didn't feel right. I started to examine myself more closely. I wanted to change but did not know how. I also had low self-esteem and peer pressure in my life. I let the social mirror dictate my life.

She Believed in Me

I wanted to shatter my reputation and build character. I was reading this book called *7 Habits of Highly Effective People* by Dr. Stephen Covey. This book was the one that the deputy director introduced into the prison system. It is a program that is geared toward the inmate changing from the inside out. One guy in the unit was speaking very highly about it. I asked Bill to send the book in to me. *It changed my life.* I do not say this lightly, but this book was life altering.

Jennifer wanted me to go to the chow hall and ask three people that I did not know (but that I have seen around) if they knew who I was. The first guy I asked said, "You are the guy that did thirteen years in the bucket for trying to escape in the trash truck."

The second man said, "You are the leader of the Aryans."

The third man that I asked said, "I do not know who you are."

I immediately said, "What do you mean you don't know who I am?" Right then and there, I knew that I had a reputation problem. Either they knew me for the thirteen years in the hole or they knew me for being the leader of the white supremacists. I would get offended if they did not know who I was. Jennifer's little test worked. I asked her to help me, and she did. I am very grateful that she invested time in helping me change my life. It is rare for anyone to take a personal interest in assisting a prisoner to become a better person. *Jennifer did this for me. She believed in me.*

For the next few months, I worked on developing a speech. I talked about my life-changing experience from participating in the VOD. I shared it with the class and anyone else that would listen to me. Then Jennifer asked for my assistance in developing a victim impact class that she wanted to teach. This class lasted only two rotations for before the administration pulled it because of a shortage of counselors.

I was worried about some of the undocumented tattoos that I had. I did not need a write-up, especially now that I was changing my life. Jennifer told me that she could help me if I were to renounce my ties to the gang. The administration considered Asatru a security threat group and had viewed it that way for years. In the federal system, Asatru is considered an Aryan hate group. It wasn't any different within the state system.

I signed renunciation papers and had all my tattoos documented. I was to have no contact or gang activity for five years. I made the decision to take my life back and to not only take it back but to also shatter that social mirror that had dictated my life all these years. I was now in danger of being killed for my stepping away and turning my back on the kindred. Blood in, blood out!

I did not tell anyone for a while about my renunciation. I also filed the paperwork for a name change. I had it printed in the local newspaper. I was Thomas Lee Fleming and not Tyrok Milosson. I thought someone would see it in there, but it did not matter to me if they did or didn't. I was on the road to taking my name back, the one my parents had given me. I had shamed that name, and it was time to make that name mean something other than hate and discontent.

It didn't take long before I received the legal documents from the courthouse. I was once again no other than Thomas Lee Fleming. I sent Mom a copy of the newspaper clipping that had my filing for a name change in it. I also sent her a copy of the court order. She was happy to learn that I was serious about changing my life.

God Has a Plan for You

I was working on a third step package for one of Dan's classes. The package was taken from an AA concept that dealt with a higher power. I was supposed to draw what I thought was my higher power on a piece of paper. I drew a scene from out my window. It was of the countryside in the springtime. I added a lake to the beautiful landscape. I always felt a bit of serenity gazing upon Mother Nature.

As I looked out my window, I saw the spring green grass covering the hillside. I also saw the first of the leaves budding on the trees. I started to cry, not knowing why at first, then I asked myself, "How could there not be a God?" As I looked out the prison window, I wondered who or what made all this beauty that was in front of me. I thought about it for a second, and I knew in my heart that there was more to it than what I had believed. The words that Bill told me that one day kept going through my head: "God has a plan for you." With tears in my eyes, I asked God into my life. My life was about to change rapidly.

It was on April 20, 2013, when I asked God into my life. How ironic, I thought. April 20 was a day that I used to celebrate when I was a heathen racist. It was the anniversary of Hitler's birthday. I used to think about that a lot, and also the fact that my grandmother was Jewish. That was something that I did not know for most of my life. Here I was with all these racial tattoos on me. Some are large swastikas. I know I can get them covered up someday, but they are reminders of who I was and how far I have come.

I think about when I entered prison and started to get all those tattoos. I did not think about my racial identity ever changing. Who would, when they were in it waist-deep? I did not ever think about hepatitis C or the possibilities of catching a disease and having it almost kill me. One thing about prison tattoos is that the odds of a person getting a disease are very high. Almost everyone I know who received tattoos in prison has hep C. Most of the men who contract the disease end up getting treatment for it. Some are successful, and some are not. I have lost a few righteous bros to liver failure. How blessed I am to be one of the few that were successfully treated for hep C!

I went to the chapel that week, and a preacher named Bill Hance was there talking about baptism. I told him that I wanted to be baptized. On May 7, 2013, three weeks after I asked God into my life, I was baptized. How was I going to tell all the Asatru men? I realized that my life would be in danger. I thought about it and came to the conclusion that I would put my life in God's hands. I went to an AA meeting where all the fellas met to talk. Since the yard was on modified lockdown, we had to find clever ways to congregate. I sat there and waited patiently for it to quiet down, and then I said, "My name is Tom, and I am an alcoholic. I have been struggling with what a higher power means to me. I finally figured it out. I am at peace now. I know who my God is. I was baptized by a preacher on May 7."

The room was really quiet. One of my former brothers got up and walked out of the room. And as he left, he punched the wall in frustration. I had just shattered his perception of me. I was his hero, his blood brother, and his friend. These men looked up to me. I was one of the founders of Asatru in the Nebraska prison system. I tried to escape, and I spent thirteen years in the hole. These are the things that prisoners admire and respect.

Another brother sitting next to me said, "Why didn't you ask me first before you did that?"

I said, "Who in the hell are you that I need to ask you anything?"

This was a brother that had been part of the inner circle of the kindred. We had spent over a year together in segregation and spent years walking and talking about life and the existence of another life after this. We had discussed and studied Hermetic philosophy and a lot of the principles of life. I liked discussing the idea of polarization and the concept of what is above, is so below. I was also aware that he knew about the escape materials that were in the locker a few years prior. I felt that if he was a friend and a true brother, he would have not allowed that to happen. He was neither a trusted friend nor a brother.

As I look back on it, I believe those conversations led me toward finding God. I searched all my life for the meaning of my existence and studied many religions and spiritual beliefs. I was active in black magic and Satanism while I was in segregation all those years ago. How can a man believe in Satan and not God? The belief that there is a creator of this world is what I have come to believe.

I endured the comments and threats on my life, but nothing ever came. I believe that my reputation and the unknown of what I was still capable of doing kept me from being assaulted. I also know that God has kept me from harm. I stood in the middle of all my enemies and smiled, waiting for the knife in the back. It never came.

I was in a self-help club that was called 7th Step. It was geared toward helping men look at their lives and preparing them for their eventual release. There was a banquet being held, and I knew that the director, Bob Houston, would be there along with the deputy director, Larry Wayne. Also along for the ride were some big shots from the community. The banquet was geared toward victim awareness. When I was about ready to go, I said a prayer. I asked God to help me find the right words to say and open the minds of the administration. I asked to be given a chance to speak with them. I was always under the assumption that the administration was against me and would never give me a fair shake. I was told by a higher-up one time that as long as the director and deputy director were in office, I would never have anything coming.

I walked into the room, and an acquaintance was standing there talking to Mr. Wayne. He called me over, and I talked with Mr. Wayne. He told me to get with him one day after a 7 Habits class. I thought, *All right, he will talk to me*. I just wanted to know if I would ever get a chance at having a job that was outside of the unit. Then as the banquet was into full swing and a couple of men had read their speeches, the guest speaker was announced. The emcee said, "Please welcome to the podium our guest speaker, Director Bob

Houston." Applause arose, and Mr. Houston took the podium. He started talking about his life and his high school. (He and I went to the same high school, ten years apart.) He then started talking about his good friend who was hurt during an escape attempt back in the early nineties. Then he talked about how his friend found closure by participating in the Victim Offender Dialogue Program. I knew he was talking about my case. Mr. Houston then said, "One of the men that took part in the escape attempt and participated in the VOD is here tonight. We even went to the same high school. I will let him tell you about it in his own words. Thomas Fleming, please come up here to the podium and share your story."

I was stunned. I stood up, walked to the podium, and shook Director Houston's hand. Then as I looked out over the big crowd, a fog settled over me. It was as if a blanket of mist covered me, and I do not remember what I was saying. I remember that at the end of my talk, the fog lifted, and I said, "Thank you." Then the crowd was clapping, and a few were wiping tears from their eyes. Director Houston shook my hand and thanked me. I returned to my seat, and a member of the parole board was sitting in the same aisle. As I walked by her, she said, "Good job, Thomas."

I looked at a dude I knew and said, "I just prayed for that!" I had just asked God to give me the words to say if I was given a chance to talk to the higher-ups. I just never thought it would be that huge of a deal, but God does big things. My faith was confirmed. All doubt was lifted. God was real. He was in my life and was answering my prayers.

I'm in 7 Habits

I knew a man that had taken 7 Habits and was a core group member. He asked me to take it. I already read the book and finished the workbook that my bro Bill had sent me from the streets. I said okay! I was in the third class, and my life was changing. I was putting it all together, from the conditioning as a child to having a belief system that was someone else's.

I had that chance to talk to Mr. Wayne after one of the classes. He was a facilitator for 7 Habits but did not get to be at every class due to his role as deputy director. We met for about an hour, and he told me that my victim had forgiven me, the State of Nebraska had pretty much forgiven me, and God has forgiven me. Then he asked me if I had forgiven myself. I had not thought of this before, and I knew I had some soul-searching to do. Then before he left, he said, "Thomas, you are a poster child for rehabilitation. You have been on the dark side of prison life, and now you are changing your life for the better." He also talked to me about how I could tell people about change better than any suit and tie could because I was living it. Once again, I felt that I was affirmed in all my decisions. I was on the right road.

I had completed the 7 Habits class with a positive attitude, and a new fire was burning in my inner being. I knew that I could make a difference in people's lives because I shared some profound lessons that I had learned over the years. I had come to the conclusion that *a man without a meaningful purpose in his life will be blown by the wind.* We all have a purpose in life. The addict's purpose is to score drugs and get high, but is that meaningful? I believe that a meaningful purpose is one that elevates the person to a higher level of life, and one that causes the ripple effect to flow forth in a positive way.

An action or cause has a result or an effect. I throw a ball up in the air and the ball will drop down. Every choice I make in life has a ripple effect in one manner or another. The day I chose to escape and hurt Mr. F, it affected him physically, emotionally, mentally, and spiritually. It affected his family, friends, coworkers, neighbors, and countless others. It affected my family and me. Even twenty-five years later, it still has an effect on my children (and now my grandchildren). They only know me from phone calls and an occasional visit. I am not there to help my sisters take care of my ailing elderly parents or to do the duties that a son should be doing. All these things have taken place because of one choice.

I grasped the 7 Habits and incorporated them in my life. I was changing my value system. One of the 7 Habit facilitators, Corporal Newell, taught the material in a way that made sense to me. He knew how the convict code was. He also knew the street attitude that most of the men in prison have. We had a connection that is hard to explain. It is taboo for an inmate to have a friendship with a correctional officer. We had one thing in common—we wanted to help the men change their thinking. Then there was Mr. Kinland. He was another facilitator in the 7 Habits for Highly Effective People. He used to be a unit manager in Tecumseh and now was a unit administer at the youth prison. He knew me from the old days when my reputation was infamous. It was a joy to watch him explain the habits in a way that was easy to comprehend. He once said, "Why should we work the habits?" Then he explained it by saying, "Because it is the right thing to do."

I was blessed to have worked with Deputy Director Larry Wayne. I was asked to be a core group member, which meant that I knew the material. I was going to be given a chance to share it with other inmates and help them change their value system. Mr. Wayne would periodically come into the class when his schedule would permit him. The 7 Habits was his baby, and he was very passionate about changing the culture of the prisons and the prison system with 7 Habits.

As I graduated the Substance Abuse Program, I was asked to remain in the unit by the program supervisor. He wanted to develop a mentor program. The men who graduated the program would live on the unit and assist the men that were in the program and help them understand and hopefully overcome addiction. One of my tasks would be to hold AA meetings and NA meetings on the unit or in one of the classrooms. It also gave me an opportunity to continue to help Jennifer with the victim impact classes.

I was also blessed to tell my story of change to every new class that started. It was rewarding to help others, but it had its price too. Whenever you have new men move onto a unit, the inmates that live there are suspicious of why they are there. The staff has been known to move a snitch onto a unit to have them inform on the activities of the other inmates that reside in the unit. We had a great group of men that wanted to be mentors, but the word was out about the SAU supervisor needing ten men to be mentors, and some of the lowlifes applied for it. One thing about living on the unit was you would get early lines. This meant you would eat first in the chow hall every meal. One problem we had was since there were women working in the unit as counselors and secretaries, some of the stalkers and perverts tried to become mentors.

    I had my reputation as a stand-up convict. This meant that the mentor program had some validity to it. I also was very up front and open about who was who in the mentor program. The supervisor was duped by a few of the undesirables who applied to be a mentor. This made it hard for the men in the program to trust us for a long time. *One thing about time, it will prove you or expose you.* A few of the mentors were exposed and booted from the program. One was a well-known snitch, and the others were known stalkers. A seasoned prisoner can tell who is on the up-and-up and who is on some bullcrap. The mentor program was a success, and some strong men would be proven and grow because of it.

    J. Keys and Josh were two men who grew in the mentor program. They had great heads on their shoulders. They developed some great classes for the students. Then there was Rueski. He was an ex-banger who was changing his ways and became a mentor. These three men became my brothers. We would eventually take the mentor program to another facility.

    I created a great relationship with all the counselors. I was asked to do some painting in Jennifer's office. I loved talking to her about life. We also discussed how the prison system could be changed to help others and lower recidivism rates. I received a job as the office porter. This meant that I would spend a few hours a day in the presence of all the counselors. I could pick their brains about why they had become substance abuse counselors. I discovered that I had a gift. I would explain through my story how I overcame addiction and also how I applied the first three steps of the twelve-step program to my life.

    As a recovering alcoholic and drug addict, I was exposed to AA when I was in my twenties. I had a conviction for driving while intoxicated. This entailed an outpatient treatment and six months of attending AA meetings. I learned the jargon of the program and all its slogans. I started to live clean and sober for about twenty months. I would go to three meetings a week at the local neighborhood meeting. I got into it so deep that I acquired a sponsor and ended up chairing a Thursday night meeting.

One thing that I did not do was turn my will and my life over to the care of a higher power. This, I would later find out, would be vital for me to stay clean. I was very antireligious at the time, being forced to go to Catholic schools all my life. I would eventually smoke pot and then go back to drinking. The final result of those choices led me to prison and my family suffering because of my choices.

Before I had God in my life, I would explain to the men in the meetings who were having a problem with the first three steps how I had come to understand the steps. The men were mostly pagans or heathens, and that was what I was at the time. I would explain to them that the first step says, "I can't do it, I have a problem, and I do not know how to handle it." The second step says, "Someone or something out there can help me." The third step says, "I will seek out that help and allow it, or them, to help me." That third step can be the program itself or a group of like-minded people. The hard part for men, especially in prison, is not only admitting they need help but asking for it. You mention God in a meeting and most of the men walk out, or they get offended.

When I found God, I really understood the third step of turning my life and my will over to his care. God has always been at the heart of AA; it was there in its beginning. I try to reach those in the meetings by sharing what my higher power has helped me do with my life and what he has done in my life. If the person approaches me after the meeting and asks me more, I hold nothing back. I love talking about what God has done in my life.

The mentor program was great for not only the residents in the program but also for the men who were mentors and were of service to others. It wasn't long before I was offered the job of cleaning the hallway that was in front of the program's door. It also happened to be the entryway for death row. This entailed cleaning the staff bathroom. I was happy because I never had a prison job that paid $3.78 a day. This was huge for me, for the simple fact that most of my pay went to arrears for child support. The more I made a day, the more I had on my account. The new warden was not a hater like his predecessor. The previous warden would not allow me to work outside of the unit or allow me a high paying job. This was the same man that was the unit administrator back at the state pen when I tried to escape. He used to bring tours to the segregation unit and stand in front of my cell door and then tell the tour how the men who tried to escape using the trash truck would never get out of the segregation unit alive.

No Peeing in the Bucket

I learned years ago that some of the good old boys would never forget, nor would they ever forgive. I had some staff tell me what a great job I was doing and that they were happy to have a clean restroom to use. I also had staff that would smear crap all over the restroom, leaving the restroom in disarray. I had a unit manager that was really down-to-earth. He supported me and even liked the job I was doing. When I would go to get my bucket of cleaning supplies that were kept in the restroom, I would discover that someone had urinated in the bucket, filling my rubber gloves up with urine. My unit manager moved the bucket into the closet that was by his office and was only accessible by the night staff. A week later, the bucket was full of urine again. I knew either I was being tested or I just had a hater. After the bucket was moved to a third location, again it was filled with urine. I knew it was a hater. I talked to Jennifer about it, and she had the unit manager have it investigated. Needless to say, the urination in the bucket had ceased. I never did learn how the investigation turned out. I talked to Jennifer because I needed to vent. I didn't know that she would have the situation investigated. I wasn't upset about it either.

The sense of humor I had was pretty cool. I did not get mad, nor did I want to seek revenge. I knew I had changed and my value system had also changed. Jennifer had made a sign up that had a cartoonish boy peeing in a bucket, and it had the red circle with a line through it. It was a "No peeing in the bucket" sign. I had it taped over the shelf the bucket was placed on. When I transferred to Omaha, I opened my big dictionary, and lo and behold, there was that sign. Jennifer had taken it and placed it in my property as a reminder of how far I had come.

One day, I was in the restroom cleaning, and I heard voices. It was the unit administrator and the deputy warden. They were talking about how shiny the waxed floor was. Then they asked me how many times I buffed the floor and how I liked my job. They even complimented me on my work. That had never happened before with the higher-ups. I just smiled. I knew something was changing. I just did not know what it was.

I stepped away from being a 7 Habits core group member. I wanted to focus on the mentor program that we started. I was called up to the captain's office so he could find out why I resigned. When I walked in the room, not only was Captain P there, but also Captain C. I explained my reasoning to them and also explained that I did not need a big audience for helping people. I felt more at peace putting all my energy into the Substance Abuse Mentor Program. Then Captain C said, "A man should not pray in the streets or in public. He should go inside his closet to pray." He had quoted a Bible verse to me that meant what I was trying to convey. I thought that was cool that the captain understood where I was coming from.

When did I start changing? I would often ask myself that question as the days, months, and years rolled on by. I signed up for program after program. I was hungry for learning the things that would help me become that man that I envisioned myself to be.

I took a course called Within My Reach and another called Inside/Out Dads. These were classes that were taught by Christian Heritage and had good instructors. The classes were geared toward relationship building and parenting skills. I learned in the Within My Reach class that my relationship skills were not good, and that I could set my own criteria on what I wanted in a relationship. I thought about these things and put together a top ten list of what I wanted in a relationship. I will not get into a relationship unless the woman meets all my expectations, or at least seven of the ten things that I am seeking in a relationship. I was never that man who thought about these things or the importance of them. No wonder my relationships never lasted! I also learned some parenting tips about listening and guiding my children. I did this more for my grandchildren. I want to be able to relate to them. I felt that I wasn't there for my children, and I want to be there for my grandchildren.

I was asked to write my testimony out for a Christian friend of mine so he could use it in the church his family goes to. I thought this was cool that someone thought my story was worth telling. After I wrote my testimony, I had copies sent into the prison. I passed these out and then had a lot of people telling me that they were using my story of change to help others. A whole new world was opening up to me.

One of the instructors for Christian Heritage was Terry O. Terry and I used to have in-depth conversations after the Inside/Out Dads classes. Terry asked me for a copy of my story because he wanted to share it with some people. A few years later, I found out that one of the teachers in the education center at the Omaha prison had read my story. She was deeply moved. Then I ended up working for her. I thought it was pretty cool that Terry shared my story with people that I had not known, and I would go on to meet those people years later.

One day in the Substance Abuse Unit, the supervisor walked in and asked me to talk to a reporter from the Pawnee newspaper. I said, "Sure." The article was on addiction and crime. These things I knew about. I did not know that the article was to be shared with the surrounding towns' newspapers. The staff members and the guards at the prison seemed to change their attitude about me. I knew something was different. I liked talking about change and my life.

I was picked to be in the Inside/Outside Criminal Justice class that would be a semester long. It would be held weekly in the education building. The class was taught by a professor that I knew. He happened to be a staff member at the state penitentiary twenty years prior when I tried to escape. He knew me and had heard the changes I was making in my life. I enjoyed sitting every week with the college students and discussing different topics about society and the criminal justice system. I did learn that I could function in a college setting. I received good grades on all my written papers and class assignments.

On one occasion, I was having a discussion about the broken prison system and the lack of victim impact classes. I also voiced my opinion about how the Department of Corrections did not advertise the Victim/Offender Dialogue Program. This individual who happened to be a staff worker at the prison asked me to write the senators at the State Capitol Building and voice my concerns. I said, "I will do one better, since I keep hearing how my story of change opens eyes. I will take my testimony and do some revamping on it so it will be something the masses can relate to and not so Christianized." I found out that my story can be a religious-themed testimony, or with some editing, it can be a message of change and forgiveness. No matter the format, the message does not change.

I asked Bill and Deb if they would get copies and send them to about fifteen senators that are in the Judiciary Committee. They said that they would love to. I never did hear back from any of the senators. I knew that my message about the lack of programming, especially victim impact classes or any programs that were geared toward victim empathy and the ripple effect of the offender's choices, was being heard.

I stood on the idea that I had made a choice, and the ripple effect of that choice was ongoing. I had become an advocate for the Victim/Offenders Dialogue Program and victim impact classes. These programs had changed my life, and if they changed my life, they could change just about anyone's life. Why weren't these programs being utilized within the Department of Corrections? I would ask this question to anyone that would listen to me. I had found my mission and something I was passion about.

I sent a copy of the testimony to the *Omaha World Herald*, which is a newspaper out of Omaha, Nebraska. I knew a girl that worked there. We had gone to high school together. I never did receive any acknowledgment that she received it. I also was told by some of my peers to send it to a reporter at Channel 6 News in Omaha. The investigative reporter wrote me back and said that Mr.

F was his friend and that he covered the escape attempt in 1991. He also said that he contacted Mr. F, and Mr. F wanted to come down and join him in visiting with me. This would be a follow-up on the Victim/Offender Dialogue that we did in 2006. It would be about how the VOD helped Mr. F with closure and also how it helped me, the inmate, change my life for the better. I was told that the administration was informed and that we were awaiting approval for all the parties to meet. I received another letter from the investigative reporter about a month later, informing me that that Department of Corrections would not approve the follow-up of the VOD because they would not have any control over what would be said. I was sad, because I really wanted to see Mr. F again. I especially wanted to thank him for helping me change my life. Priceless! I still believe that if that meeting would have taken place, it would have helped victims become aware that there is a program that can help them find closure. It would also help the inmates find some accountability, only if they had the testicular fortitude to face the results of their actions.

9

Do I Want to Go Where, Sir?

"Mr. Fleming, here is a pass. You are to report to turnkey immediately," the caseworker said.

I was thinking, *Hell no, I knew I didn't violate any rules. I hope my mom is okay.* Anytime you're called up to turnkey unexpectedly, you fear that it is news about a family member passing away. I sat there for about thirty minutes in the vestibule awaiting someone to come and tell me why I was summoned to turnkey. I looked up, and there stood Captain P, holding the door open for me.

He said, "Come on back to my office. I have a question for you."

I thought, *What the hell is this about?* I had my guard up because I did not know what he was going to ask me.

He said, "All those tattoos you have, I want to know if you have any Hells Angel ties?"

I said, "My second cousin is a patch holder, sir, and I grew up idolizing them. They were in my neighborhood, and they were my role models, sir."

He said, "Those are swastikas on you, and the one that says 100% Peckerwood, are you a part of that peckerwood gang?"

"No, sir. Those kids are a product of the new school of thought. What I believed was old-school. I also believe they are lost and that they have no concept of preserving their own kind. I can go on and on, but I won't, sir. I believe I've answered your question. What is this all about? You already know the answer to these questions, sir. You also know I have renounced my ties to the white supremacists and have changed my value system. I walk what I talk, and I was teaching this in 7 Habits, and I am teaching this in the SAU mentor program."

He said, "I had a talk with Deputy Director Larry Wayne, and he wants me to ask you one question. Do you want to transfer to the Omaha Correctional Center? I need an answer right away so we can get the paperwork going."

I sat there in shock. I was lost for words, and all I could think about was how happy Mom would be to know I had worked my way out of the maximum prison where I thought I would spend the rest of my life at.

A tear formed in my eye, and it started to roll down my cheek. The captain sat there and smiled. I was so confused. I said, "Yes, sir! I will go to OCC. Why do they want me in Omaha, may I ask?" He proceeded to tell me that the SAU supervisor was taking the job of supervisor of the Substance Abuse Unit in Omaha and could use my help starting a mentor program there. There was also a need for me in 7 Habits as a core group member. All he had to do was inform the deputy director that I said yes.

It seemed that I met all the criteria for a transfer. I was numb and did not know what to think. My life as I knew it was about to change even more. I was told that it would be a few days before the paperwork would be ready for me to sign. I thanked the captain and made my way back to the housing unit.

I went and lay down on my bunk and started to cry. I was in shock and couldn't think straight. I thanked God for answering once again another one of my prayers.

I always wanted to go to Omaha and be close to my family, but I was transferred to the maximum-security prison in Tecumseh for a reason. I was serving a 44- to 117-year prison sentence for committing violent crimes. It took a while for all this to sink in. Was this for real? Am I dreaming all of this? Why me? Then I answered myself with why not me? Haven't I changed my life? Here I am helping others who are struggling with addiction. I shattered my reputation and built character deep within my core. I practiced what I preach in every part of my life. I have been speaking to the high school and

THE RIPPLE EFFECT

college classes that tour the prison, telling them my story and sharing with them how Mr. F instilled forgiveness in me and helped me turn my life around. I was deserving of this transfer. I smiled and couldn't wait to call Mom.

"Have I thanked you lately?" I said.

"No, for what?" Mom asked.

"For having such a beautiful baby boy," I said.

Mom laughed. It was a laugh from deep down in her heart. I would do this periodically to her. I love to make her smile. I thought about the entire heartache I have caused her over the course of my life, and it does not feel good. I have made it part of my mission to have her always smile and never do anything in my life to ever embarrass her or bring shame to the family name ever again.

I said, "Are you sitting down, Ma?"

She said, "Yes, I am. I am always sitting in my chair."

I said, "Good. I have something I need to tell you."

"What is wrong?" Ma asked.

I said, "Nothing, Ma. All is alright with the world. I was just told that I am being transferred to Omaha and should be there in about ten days."

All I heard was Mom crying, and it was good to hear tears of joy in her voice. This solidified that I had been changing and have become the man that she always wanted me to be. She could not believe that I was being transferred to the Omaha prison, nor could I.

I called my son Thomas Jr. and his wife, Ani, and told them that I was on my way to Omaha. They were elated. My daughter Holly was in shock. She could not believe it. She grew up thinking that I would never get out of prison because that was what her mother always told her. It was good to hear my grandchildren giggle on the phone when I called them, but now I would be ten minutes from their homes, so visits would be easier and cheaper for them. I did not like visits very much, only because I knew it cost my family a lot of money in gas to make the trip from Omaha to Tecumseh and then back. Then they had to have money for the vending machines, not so much for me but for those little ones. I used to love drinking chocolate milk with the grandbabies. It was our thing to share a bottle and make faces after every drink. The memories of those prison visits are embedded in my heart. *My dream of getting out one day seemed to be starting to become a reality.*

I had sent my story of change and the need for victim awareness classes to an advocate for prison reform, and he informed me that he forwarded it to the *Nebraska Criminal Justice Review*. This is a prison newsletter that is delivered to all the prisons in the state, as well as prison officials and the general public. In my article, I talked about who I am and what led me to prison. I then talked about my crimes and how I was one of the founders and leaders of Asatru, which was a pagan religion deeply mired in racism. I explained how a couple of lifers approached me when I was scouting out the trash truck, which eventually allowed me to join their escape plans. The *NCJR* newsletter editor wrote me, asking permission to print my article in the *NCJR*. I said that I approved, and it was printed. It came out the first week of August 2014.

I had a lot of guys thank me for sharing my story. They thought it was brave of me to talk about my change and the things I went through. It also gave them courage to open up about their own change or lack thereof. I also had some men that did not like the idea that I called Asatru a racial hate group. I am standing by my words and will not lie about the truth as I lived it. The prison officials have given it the title of a white supremacy threat group. I had one friend that was convicted for conspiracy to escape in the 1991 trash truck fiasco get mad at me because I said that a couple of lifers approached me and asked me to be part of their escape attempt. I will not sway from the truth, no matter who does or doesn't like it or agree with it.

I was slandered for my comments, and my life was threatened. I just smiled and held my head high. This was a big breakthrough for me. I stood up to the peer pressure, and I did not allow the social mirror to dictate how I conducted my life. I took charge of my own life for the first time and did not care about what others thought.

I had an Asatru member who was picking up trash come up to me as I was washing windows one day and asked me if I was going to Omaha. I smiled and asked him why he was whispering. Then I asked him why he was talking to me all secretly. Before he could answer me, I told him that I already knew the answer to my own questions. He was not supposed to speak to me. The kindred forbid everyone associated with them not to speak to me. I smiled because of the hypocrisy that was being shown. A grown man hiding his talking to me and breaking his own rules by doing so. I just thought, *Poor Yippee!*

I wondered how many men over the years under my leadership had done things that were forbidden by the rules. I knew in my heart that I made the right decisions in my life. I was free of others' opinions and thoughts about me. I stopped being a people pleaser. I was my own man, and I liked myself.

The warden came down to the housing unit to tell me that everything was cleared for me to be transferred to Omaha. I said my goodbyes to the bros who stayed true to our friendship. It was hard to leave those men that I had spent over a quarter of a century with. I had friends that I had fought side by side with and friends that I spent years living next to in the segregation units. I have men that I had cried with when they lost one of their parents or loved ones. Men whom I had shared advice with and walked mile after mile next to on the prison yard. I think about all the men that I have lived next to in the concrete jungle that existed in the middle of nowhere.

I was about to walk away and not see some of these true brothers again. Some of them, like my brother Nose, would die inside of the fences. Nose died four months after I left Tecumseh. He is sadly missed but not forgotten. It was hard saying goodbye. My bro Crow was that one brother I didn't want to leave behind. We spent the last twenty-five years together. Through thick and thin, we were bros. We partied together, shared our hopes and dreams with each other, and we even tried to escape together. This ended up with us in the segregation unit together for years. I even shed a tear when I said my goodbyes to Dan and Jennifer and the counselors in the Substance Abuse Unit.

From 2002 until 2014, I resided in Tecumseh. Now it was time to say goodbye and get on to the next chapter of my life. I stood in the intake room, waiting to get strip-searched and chained up for the ride to Omaha. I was nervous as hell. I was nervous because I was going to a minimum-security prison where there were no lockdown units and there was an open yard. This was something that I have not had in a lot of years. I also knew that the staff did not know who I was as a person but only knew me by name and reputation. I anticipated some hassling when I got there.

I walked down the long corridor to the state van that was waiting to take me on down the highway. I walked out the door and stepped up to the running board to get in the van. I stopped and looked around at the fences and the buildings. I took a deep breath, exhaled, and smiled. I bent my torso over to get inside of the van. The guard reached over me and attached the seat belt. I was ready for the ride. It is state law that everyone must be strapped in their seats. This was a law that I had not thought about for over a quarter of a century.

The gate opened, and the van backed up. We were on our way. There were two other inmates with me that were being transferred to Omaha. We did not talk because it was a surreal experience to be leaving the Tecumseh prison. This was a big moment in our lives, leaving a maximum prison and going to a minimum-security prison. It is hard to explain the relief a man has when he leaves a place of little hope and a lot of negativity, only to go to a place where almost everyone has hope and a release date.

Northbound and Down

The van pulled onto Highway 50 and headed north. I looked back at the prison one more time and told myself that I would never walk back into that prison again unless it was as a visitor. I know that I want to be that poster child for rehabilitation and will be going back to prison as a man who changed and succeeded in society. I am that man who shares his story with other inmates, and I show them that there is a way out of prison that is honorable, and that a man can still be an asset to his community and help others.

We traveled down the highway. It was a two-lane road until we changed lanes and got onto Interstate 80 and headed east. This stretch of interstate was on the outskirts of Omaha. I could not believe my eyes. I had not been to Omaha in almost thirty years, and I did not recognize it. The road was four lanes, and the cars and trucks were going fast. We were in the middle lane, and I was sitting next to the window. A truck was to the left of us, and a truck was to the right. I felt helpless as the van swayed back and forth. The trucks were right next to me as I looked out the window. I was very intimidated by the traffic and very nervous.

Here I was, a man who had spent over twenty-five years living with killers and violent men, and I found myself intimidated by highway traffic. The scenery was very different than I remembered it. The farmlands were now buildings. Businesses were everywhere, and it looked like business was booming in Omaha. The landscape was unrecognizable to me. I felt as if I was a foreigner in a strange land. As the van headed deeper into the city, I started to see exits that I used to take back in the eighties when I was a free man. I recognized some parts of south Omaha where I was born and raised. That feeling and excitement of coming home started to hit me, and I felt a tear start to form in my eye. I thought I would never see my south Omaha again.

The van pulled up to the east gate, and I was right there next to the river. There was the old railroad bridge that spanned over the Missouri River. I used to go fishing under that bridge but on the Iowa side of the river with my uncle Rich when I was a youngster. For some odd reason, I felt as if I were home.

The gate opened, and the van pulled into the prison and up to the walkway. I saw that were there were six guards waiting. This was the welcoming committee. I thought at least they showed unity through numbers. I knew this was a statement to me that said they were not supportive of me being here. I exited the van and was escorted into the visiting room, where I was be strip-searched and processed in.

As soon as I was in the shakedown room, I started to strip down to nothing. The door opened, and in walked a captain. He stood there, looked at me with a cold stare, and said, "Mr. Fleming, do you remember me?" I looked at him and could not place him. I looked at his name tag, and my mind flashed back twenty years to when I was in South Forty. This was not good, I thought.

I said, "I do remember you, Captain. Nice to see you again."

He gave me that once-over and mumbled something about his staff and no harm would come to them as he walked off. I knew that these people did not want me here, and it would take me a while to prove to them that I was no longer a threat. I had that feeling way before I even stepped off the van that I would have to start all over again. All these people knew was that violent man that assaulted one of theirs while trying to escape, and they did not want me on their yard.

I waited for my property to be searched by the property clerk. He took a lot of my property, and I was confused about it. I thought how I was allowed certain things like gum and tape at a maximum prison but not at a minimum prison. They could have all my stuff. I did not care. I was in Omaha and close to my mother.

I sat in a room waiting to see the man that was in charge of my processing in. It was another staff member that worked at the state penitentiary back in the day. He told me that I had a fresh start here at OCC, but eyes would be upon me. If any of his staff were harmed in any way, it would not bode well for me. I told him that I wanted to be judged by my actions, not by my past. I also explained to him that *time would prove me or expose me*. I went through the other questions that pertained to any enemies or if I was going to hurt myself. I was thinking about where these people came up with these crazy questions. The mental health lady told me if I needed any mental health counseling that I could put in a request form. I smiled, arose, and went to get my property. I was officially logged into the Omaha Correctional Center.

As I pushed a cart across the yard containing all my property, heads turned. I could see guys talking to each other and point in my direction. A few yelled, "Hey, Big T, good to see you!" Just like that, I was in my new home. I had an attitude about calling prison home. I came to the conclusion a long time ago that *where I lay my head was home*. I heard that in a Metallica song. I thought that that was as close to the truth as it could get. Think about it, my body and my mind is all I have. Wherever I am at any given time. So if I am in a three-bedroom house or a two-bedroom apartment, I lay my head on a pillow and call it home. If I am in a house trailer or a jail cell, I still lay my head down and reside there in mind, body, and spirit. I have lived in a prison cell for over half my life. I am now fifty-six years old and in my thirty-first year of incarceration. *Where I lay my head is home.*

I walked into the housing unit and looked around. I was to share a cell with this dude that was about my age. He was doing county time for domestic assault. That was not cool with me. I felt that I could handle it.

I tried to put a key in the keyhole. "This damn thing is bent," I said. Nothing was wrong with the key. It was me that was screwed up. It had been about thirty years since I had used a key. Just a little out of practice, I thought.

I went out to the open yard after I put my property in the cell. This was the only open yard in the state. All the other prisons were on lockdown and only had modified movement. An open yard means that you can walk the yard and do pretty much what you want while the yard is open. The yard is only shut down for count time twice a day and is open until 8:30 p.m. This was something that I was not able to do for a couple of years at Tecumseh's prison. I walked right up to one of the many trees that were on the yard, and I hugged it. I laughed like a kid.

For many years, I daydreamed about sitting under a tree and shooting the bull with my friends. I also used to think how it would be nice to lay back in the grass again. I pondered for quite a while to try to remember the last time I sat in the grass under a tree. These were things that I had only dreamed of over the past couple of decades. When I spent all those years in segregation, I thought a lot about the trees and the grass. I used to have dreams about them. I was separated from them for a long time. A person existing in the outside world rarely gives any thought about walking on grass or being close to a tree. Some things in life are taken for granted. It isn't until a person is separated from these things for a long time, then the ache kicks in and the longing for these things hurt deeply.

Here I was in Omaha, not even two hours, and I had already used a key, petted a three-legged dog, and hugged a tree. Life was good, for a few minutes anyway. The population is very absent-minded when it comes to respect. I found out that respect was lacking within the mindset of the population here in Omaha. The normal inmate was doing short time. It was like a merry-go-round ride for them. In one month and out the next. Mostly everyone here did not do hard time in a maximum-security prison.

This prison was full of short-timers that were doing a couple of years at the most and were here for their first number. There were a lot of parole violators here too. When you have a population that comes and goes like a revolving door, it sets up a mindset of instant gratification. Most of these men spent their time getting high. They were working on their next number even before the one they were serving was done. This reminded me of myself. I did the same things on my first trip to prison in the eighties. If I could go back and talk some sense into that young man who thought he had it all figured out, would he have listened? He didn't know squat.

Bloom Where You Are Planted

Prison is the long-term consequence of a short-term gratification. I have only looked out for my addiction and have not thought of the consequences of those actions. I got high, robbed a gas station, and got caught. Wow! Thirty years for that choice. Didn't see that coming. Instant gratification does have a price. Many a man has not even given it a thought. I see so many men falling out on K-2, a synthetic drug that is supposed to act like marijuana. These men think that because the drug does not show up on a urinalysis test that they are free to use it. The sad thing is watching these men drop to the ground and see their heart stop beating. The medical staff haul them off to the hospital, and they get resuscitated. Two days later, they are back on the yard smoking it again. They lose good time and do not care. Why? Maybe the answer is that their time was short to begin with. They leave for work release and are back within a week for violating rules, usually for getting high. Once they are released back into society, they are usually returned to jail for new crimes. It is sad to see self-gratification in action. I was that man who threw it all away for that self-gratification and did not learn at first. *I applaud the men who have the testicular fortitude to say enough is enough and want something different in their lives.*

I firmly believe that until a man is ready to be accountable for all his actions and not blame anyone but himself for his predicament, he will not succeed. Not a lot of men in prison can face the truth of the matter. A lot of them fall into peer pressure and can't say no. Until a man says, "I have had enough and want something different in my life," he will always be on the fence. It is really hard to stand up in front of your peers and say, "I am done. I do not want to spend the rest of my life in prison."

I have heard a lot of men over the years say that they miss their kids and that their kids are their life. I often say to those men that their kids did not mean anything to them, because they took care of their self-gratification ahead of those kids. I did this myself, so I know from experience. If those kids were our lives, we would be out their making their lives a little better than our lives have been. Instead, we were wrecking their lives. They ended up being the ripple effect of our actions. Those kids are growing up without a father in their lives, without a role model in the home. *Long-term separation is a result of a short-term gratification.*

I walked the yard for a few days, and my legs were sore from the lack of use at Tecumseh. I would get up and make myself a cup of coffee then go to this certain bench that faced the Missouri River. There I would watch the sunrise and see the beautiful colors that bounced off the morning clouds. Then there were turkeys that lived on the riverbank. There was lot of them, and they roamed the fence lines. It is a site to see them roost in the trees and then jump down in the morning. I thought that I was very blessed to be here in Omaha.

I got a job on the bucket crew picking up trash and mowing lawns. I enjoyed my job very much. The boss knew my past and was willing to give me a chance. I thought that was very cool of him. I still had a little bit of that conspiracy motive running through my thoughts. The good old boys were still out to get me. One thing that I could not shake was this feeling that they would send me back to Tecumseh at any given moment. I was a bit paranoid, to say the least.

I thought about going back because I had a hard time adjusting to the disrespect that was running amok in the prison.

I thought about this for a while and tried to figure out why these people were acting that way. I came to the conclusion that there was no effective leadership among the gangs. I witnessed some youngsters preying on the weak. I was disgusted with what I was witnessing. I was not that guy anymore, so why did I even care? I found out that here in OCC, you can be anything you want to be. There were men here who were on protective custody at Tecumseh and others that were on PC at the state penitentiary. Now they were running a gang, self-proclaimed shot callers. I thought about how odd this prison was, and I needed to be careful and not stick my nose where it did not belong. The leader in me wanted to straighten out these lost men and get them to act right.

I witnessed a man preaching to others the importance of preserving their race then turn around and go into an elderly inmate's cell and steal everything the man had. This elderly man was of the same race as the ones that were beating the racial propaganda drum. How lost they are, and how sad this made me. I did have the opportunity to voice my opinion to one of the youngsters that was in charge. He knew my son and also knew who I was. I do not know if it did any good talking to him, but I had to tell him how disgusted I was with what I was witnessing. Then I told him of my change and how I became the man I am today.

A planter of seeds I have become, and I would talk to whoever asked what had happened to me. I had a lot of men talk to me about how they wanted out of the gang life but did not want the problems it would cause them to renounce their ties. Blood in and blood out was how the game was played. A lot of these kids come into prison their first time and want to belong to something. Some join because their friends are in it; others join because if they don't, they are threatened with going to protective custody. Life in prison has changed so much that I feel like I am part of a dying breed, an old dinosaur.

I had finally found my place in OCC. I believe it is my place to be that light of change and to show everyone that change is possible. I can live with the disrespect around me. I am above it, and I have learned that I do not have to react. I can respond. I have a choice! It is my responsibility to show the youngsters that they, too, have a choice.

One of the core group members came to me and asked me if I was ready to start being a 7 Habits core group member again. I did not hesitate and said yes. Josh also came aboard as a core member. All the fellas were back together again. We also had Corporal Newell and Mr. Kinland as instructors; they were the best. I was blessed to be able to not only work with them but also learn from them. When the four of us were working together core group members, we were in sync. We had this knack to work off each other and get the class to really understand where we were coming from and also to be able to apply the material to their lives. We had a strong two years together as a team from 2014 to 2016.

The Boys Are Back in Town

I was called to the unit manager's office and was told that the supervisor wanted to speak with me in his office, which was over in the chapel. I went over to his office, and we discussed what my role in the substance abuse mentor program would be. He wanted to start the mentor program here at OCC immediately. I was given full reigns and only needed to find a few like-minded individuals who wanted to make a difference here in this prison that was overrun with addicts. I was to move into an eight-man cell in a few days, and this was a nightmare for me. I had just gotten used to living with one cellmate, and now I would have to deal with seven other personalities.

There were a few other good mentors here in OCC that were very involved in helping start the mentor program in Tecumseh. I needed to talk to them and see if they were on board. This would be hard because no one wanted to live in an eight-man cell. I knew my friend Josh from Iowa was interested and couldn't wait to get the okay to move. He was living with an active addict who was smoking K-2 every night in his cell. I told him in a few days, we were going to make the move, and he was happy.

I talked to my bro Rueski, and he was apprehensive about it and was struggling with some other issues but would let me know. I knew I would have to work hard to get him, but it would be worth it in the end. To make a long story short, Rueski made some life-changing decisions while in the mentor room. He walked into prison a young kid and walked out as a great respectable man.

Then there was J. Keys. This brother was in my group at Tecumseh's substance abuse unit. We had the same group counselor, Mr. Dan. J. Keys was a Christian, and his pops was and still is a great preacher and a respected man around the country. So Keys had a lot of positive influence in his life. Keys, Josh, Rue, and I made the mentor program at Tecumseh what it was, and it was successful. If I could get all these dudes in the same room, I knew we could put together a solid mentor program again.

I moved in the substance abuse unit, a.k.a. SAU in September 2014, about six weeks after coming to OCC. Josh moved in about two hours after me, and we were the first ones in the room with a few good men already in there, but they were waiting to graduate. There were a few others, but they still smoked dope, and I knew it would be a trust thing right from the start. There was another recovering addict in the cell called Big Rob. I could tell right away that he was the cell boss. Every cell had that alpha male in it, and Rob was the dude in A-13.

I sat back and did what I always do—keep cool and let the rest of the men slowly find out who I was. It didn't take long, and I was talking to them on their level. I told them that I did not come here to change them or to tell on them. Telling was not in my DNA. I did not complain when they stayed up late talking because they were too high to sleep.

I talked to Jason who was once living in the cell with Rob to come on aboard as a mentor. Jason is a devout Christian and works a recovery program. He also knows all the staff in the SAU. So we were introduced to the staff at the weekly unit meeting. There were rumors that we were put into the program to snitch on the men in the program. I used empathic listening skills that I had learned in 7 Habits to understand where all this hate was coming from. We dealt with it at Tecumseh and had to go through it again here at OCC. I know from experience that a man will tear down what he does not understand. I did it myself, and so did all the men that I led. If you wanted to change and do something better with your life, well, that is not cool in prison, and you must be working with the man. I have heard all the rhetoric before and knew what I had to do. I was on a mission to change that stereotype.

We stood in front of all the men that were in the program. About ninety men were in attendance. It did not help the situation when the unit manager of the housing unit introduced us as mentors and said that he was going to clean up the unit. Okay! I thought, *Hell, I need to straighten this crap up fast. I am not here to clean anyone's unit up.* When they asked us to introduce ourselves, everyone looked at me, so I figured I would be the alpha male, so to speak.

I said, "Hey, my name is Tom, and I am an addict. I also am a mentor, and I live in A-13. I have a three-seven number, which means I have been around for about thirty years. I am the man who tried to escape and did thirteen years straight in the hole. I also went through the Victim Offender Dialogue Program and have changed my life. This does not mean I get down wrong. It simply means I have no room in my life for dope or stupid decisions. I am tired of prison and want to do something better with my life. If any of you want to change or want something different in your life, then holler at me. If you do not want to change, holler at me anyway. You may need a couple of batteries for a light. I won't turn you down." All the men in the room clapped, and I believe that my point was made.

I received word that someone was saying foul things about me. First thought wrong as the saying goes. I went into that buried vault for a second, and it was nothing nice. It is not hard to make a prison shiv if you use your imagination. The thought of hurting the person did cross my mind a time or two. I firmly believed that I was and am on a higher plane of existence. I reverted back to all the lessons I have learned in my life, and this was the time to put it all into practice. I valued a principle that I used before, and it is worth repeating. *Time will either prove you or it will expose you.* I knew in my heart and deep within my soul that I have been proven. I am a changed man.

As the days rolled on by, more and more men realized that we were not their enemy. We were only there to show them that change was possible. I used my reputation as a tool instead of a weapon. I believe I was able to reach a lot of youngsters and teach them about changing their thinking. I had to gain their trust first. Gaining the trust of anyone in prison is hard. Men always glorified the hardened convict. I knew I could get them to trust me by being honest and forthright.

Keys and Rue came aboard as mentors, and Rue had a reputation as a gang member who had been around since he was a teenager. Keys had a reputation in the pot scene as a big mover and shaker. He is also known for his musicianship. Josh was a veteran and well respected. He had a gift for organizing things and explaining things in a way everyone could understand. We had put together a strong and solid mentor program.

Josh, Keys, Rue, and I were given the green light to teach a program called Psychology of Incarceration by Khalil Osiris. This was to be designed by weekly DVD viewing and discussions. The main objective was for us to explain the seven domains that Mr. Osiris talked about. These domains focused on changing your thinking and preparing yourself for release. Mr. Osiris had done about twenty calendars in the federal system. When he was released, he faced a lot of difficulties and developed a way to stay out of prison and help others overcome those difficulties. To get a head start in life by focusing on building your strengths and overcoming your weaknesses while you are still incarcerated will help a person significantly. The classes were weekly, and there was a limit to how many people could be in the class. The room we were given was small, so that meant the class would be small. The signup sheet was full every time it was put up. This was great to see.

I held 7 Habit reviews with the men who were in SAU and enrolled in 7 Habits. The 7 Habits class was on Wednesdays. Every Wednesday morning, I would get my cup of coffee and put my books on the table in the dayroom, then wait for the men to show up. It was good to have five men around a table discussing how they were changing their paradigms. It also attracted others into the discussions and into enrolling in the next 7 Habits class. Rueski got involved with me to keep his saw sharpened. It was rewarding to spend quality time in prison by helping others discover their weaknesses and watch them make life-changing decisions.

A few men were already holding N/A meetings and AA meetings in the classroom that was available in the evenings. Rob and Jason were two of the mentors who lived in the room. They were heavily involved in chairing the nightly meetings. A few men started Bible study classes in the room after the recovery meetings. The mood in the unit was changing.

There were still men getting high in the bathroom stalls. It was a challenge to stand around in a roomful of smoke while you were showering. I just smiled and minded my own business, just like I have for the past thirty years. It has kept me safe thus far. I used to not like waiting to use the toilet. There were two toilets and one urinal for over sixty men on the tier. Always a line, and a person had to always bleach the toilet before using it. I never did get used to living in that dorm-room setting.

The Garden of Trust

I was asked to upgrade from the bucket crew to the garden crew. This meant I would be working in the grounds shop all day and toil in the big vegetable garden. I was in seventh heaven. It was fall, and the garden was winding down. I was able to eat fresh tomatoes right off the vine. The peppers I ate were hot, and I mean hot. The fellas were able to grow reapers and ghost peppers. I kept busy. There was still one more round of cutting the prison yard's grass. The boss, Mr. Thompson, was a cool dude who looked out for his crew. I was standing there by the lawn mowers, and he came up and told me to go get two gas cans out of the locked cabinet that he had just opened. I walked up and grabbed two full five-gallon cans of gas. I was directed to fill the lawn mowers. I just stood there and looked at him. I thought I was being set up. I said to him, "Did you forget what I got eighty years for?"

He laughed and said, "This is not a setup, and I know you did not light anyone on fire, and I trust you. If I didn't, you wouldn't be back here." I loved my job.

The mechanic asked me to help him remove the gas tank from the Z-Trak. This was a zero-radius turning lawn mower that had two levers for controls. We had the gas tank out and had all the gas poured into five-gallon buckets while we worked on the tank. I was lying on the ground under the machine while the mechanic was over it, positioning the gas tank back into position. I was putting the bolts back in when I saw a lieutenant and a sergeant enter the shop. They were asking my boss why it smelled like gas. The boss told them that he had us working on the tank, and it should be done soon. They looked at me and then at the mechanic. They did not say anything. They just turned around and left. The boss came over and said some people were still nervous about me working in the shop. He smiled and walked back to his office. The boss was a cool dude, and I knew that he was helping me tear down that old stereotype.

A lot of guards only knew me by name and were really paranoid about me being in OCC, and especially about me working around gas and tools. I learned that not everyone was against me. I would go the extra mile for the boss because he was going the extra mile for me.

One of my coworkers told me the boss wanted him and me to go cut the ballfield grass one time before winter set in. The grass had slowed down and was not growing much. I got on the John Deer Tractor, a 335 model. It was a blast to drive. I took off to the ballfield to cut the grass. The other guy was on the Z-Trak, and it was faster than the 335. He took the bigger part of the ballfield, and I had the side field. I was in heaven. The thrill of sitting on a machine and driving was something that I never in a million years thought I would be doing. I couldn't quit smiling as I drove around the ballfield and watched the airplanes land and take off from the airport.

The prison was right next to the airport. I would stand in the garden periodically and watch a big plane come in from the east and drop its landing gear to land. I would watch it all the way until the tires touched the strip and a puff of smoke or dust would rise up. I could stand there for hours, watching the planes take off and land.

It took me back to my childhood days when my uncle Gary would take me to the road that was behind the airport. We would sit on the hood of his car, and the planes would be fly right over us as they landed. It was cool to have a plane that close to you while it flew over. The old airport road is no longer accessible since the Twin Towers were flown into. The Homeland Security made it impossible to get close to the airport.

It had rained, and the boss wanted to get that last cut in. This made it a little hard to maneuver the mowers. I loved it because here I was, in my fifties and pushing a mower like it wasn't anything. I did not ask for a relief the whole time we were cutting the yard. Many men that get on the bucket crew have a hard time working hard. I knew a lot of the guys that were on the bucket crew for the easy money. When it came to mowing lawns or shoveling the snow, they needed help or just did not show up to work. The norm was that they would work all summer, and when winter arrived, they would quit. I took pride in the fact that I could outlast these youngsters when it came to hard labor. I remember when that judge sentenced me, he said, "Thirty years, hard labor." I always wondered why he said that, because the one thing about prison is *it is not hard labor.*

In prison, most men have cake jobs their whole sentence. I was a table wiper when I went to prison the first time. Then I cleaned showers for a bit. I did work in the woodshop for over a year in the eighties. That was when I met Curly Wolf. I had a lot of jobs that dealt with cleaning and most of the men in prison clean. The pot and pan washing job was good. I was able to eat all the time. *My whole point is that a man does not have to work hard if he doesn't want to.* The hard labor and busting rocks all day era has been gone for a lot of years. So when the judge said, "Hard labor," I had to smile inside.

I was asked to till the side garden. This would be the first time in my life that I used a tiller. I had a small tiller back in the day, but it was more like a weed eater that scratched the surface. I fired it up and put it in gear. It took off. This thing jumped five feet with me hanging on to it for dear life. I stalled it, and I heard a lot of laughing going on behind me. The whole crew and the boss were watching me. "Get your giggle on," I said, laughing myself. I was having a blast and learning to do things that I had never done or experienced in my life.

I think back on it, and I see how blessed I am to be able to do these things. I was helping the mechanic tear the lawn mowers apart and rebuild the carburetors. Then the boss asked me if I knew how to paint, and I said, "Yep. As a kid I helped my grandpa paint houses, inside and out." I walked up to the maintenance shop and picked up a five-gallon bucket of paint and a few brushes, along with the other accessories that I would need to paint the shop with. I was now a painter. It was winter, and the garden was empty. We had to keep busy during the slow time.

I painted that whole shop that winter, and it looked really nice and fresh. When the snow hit, it hit hard. We did a lot of shoveling. I would get woken up at 4:00 a.m. to go out and clean the walkways before the shift change at 6:00 a.m. I loved standing in the yard in the middle of the night with hardly anyone around and enjoyed the quietness. I was on the wakeup roster with the other workers. We would get up and put salt out. We were hard workers, and I loved every aspect of my job. One snowfall, I was on the snowblower, and that was fun. Also driving the 335 with a little plow attached to it was a blast to drive.

When springtime rolled around, we would go up in the loft and set up grow lights and tables. We would plant seeds that were harvested from the previous year's garden. The boss would also purchase seeds and young plants to add to what we had already started in the loft. To plant a seed and then tend to the plant until it grows big enough to harden, and when the time is right, put it in the ground. Doing these things gave me a sense of pride and satisfaction. I felt that my life was complete or as complete as it could be in prison.

I Pray Crow Is Okay

Breaking news hit the TV. I was kicked back in the cell when the news said that a riot broke out at the Tecumseh State Correctional Institution. Two inmates killed. Then the newsman talked about a housing unit being burned down. Keys, Josh, Rue, and I had just left there. I left in August 2014, and the riot broke out on Mother's Day in May 2015. I prayed for all my friends and hoped they were safe.

My bro Crow was safe. I had found out that he was not in the housing unit that was burned down. That was a relief. I knew that all those guys there were doing hard time, a lot harder than it previously had been. This meant that they were on complete lockdown with no movement. I found out that they went days without showers and had to eat sack lunches in their cells for a couple of months.

The ripple effect from the riot hit the other prisons. All our laundry that was being washed at TSCI was now being washed here at OCC. The way the OCC prisons laundry was set up would not handle the daily loads. They only operated using two washers and two driers. There were seven hundred inmates that turned in a lot of bags to be washed every day. Our clothes would come back wet most of the time. Working in the garden meant that not all the dirt in my work clothes would be washed out. Almost everyone's whites were dingy gray. A man just didn't feel clean after taking a shower and putting on dingy clothes.

I believe the riot brought those of us here that did time at TSCI a little closer. I would have profound conversations with Rue about change and making the right decisions in life, no matter the circumstances. I know that each of us had friends still at TSCI. The riot impacted everyone.

10

Providing Catalyst for Change

Rueski would come in from the shower, sit down, and ramble on about God and spirituality. He would then change the subject in the middle of the conversation. I would talk to him because I would never give up on anyone. I was the same way and had friends in my life who never gave up on me. Mom never gave up and always knew there was some good in me somewhere. My bro would come back from the shower higher than a kite, and it became a regular thing. As a mentor living in the mentor room, I told him that it was not right for him to smoke dope in front of these men and then try to help them overcome their addictions. That was duplicity at its finest. My bro finally figured it out. He stepped up, straightened his life out, and became one of the best mentors there was.

This act of recognizing a weakness and asking for help to overcome that weakness was what we were all about as mentors. My bro got back into his relationship with Christ, and I was a witness to the power of belief. Rue was like a son to me, and we had that special bond that two bros have when you can be there through all your trials and tribulations. He finally had the Violent Reduction Program taken off his parole plan. He was set a hearing for parole. He went on to work release, got married to a nice Swedish woman, and eventually paroled out.

I got word that he was doing great and he was working hard at two jobs. I am so proud of him. I am grateful that I was able to be there for him as a friend and a brother. The day that Rue was to leave for work release, I told him goodbye with tears rolling down my face. It was hard keeping it together. I never felt that way watching another brother leave.

My bro Keys and I become really close too. I would tell him that he would make a great preacher one day. He loves the Lord but does not want to preach, and that is something I hope he embraces one day. He is a family man, and one thing that stuck out with me as I listened to him in the 7 Habits classes was how he shared his experience of empathic listening skills with the men in the class. He explained how he changed his whole paradigm after applying the habit of *seek first to understand then to be understood.*

As friends in the mentor room, we became sounding boards for each other. We had profound conversations about God, life, family, and our existence in the world. He was eventually sent to work release and then returned to prison as a guest for a Metro Community class called *Employability Skills*. He shared his experiences with the fellas. He told them that he took a low-paying job sewing in a factory. He learned how to sew in the prison sewing shop. He took that job, and after some prayer and not giving up, he found a job at a company that fabricated metal for all types of projects. He started out at a good wage, and after a few months, he joined the union, and now he made real good money. Not bad for just getting out of prison.

Keys changed his value system. *He is living proof that a man can change from an inside/out approach.* Changing your values will result in changing your thinking. Once your thinking has changed, your behavior and attitude will change. Then your choices will change to match your core beliefs. Every choice you make has a consequence. A good value system ends up with positive results.

One man that started the mentor program with us at Tecumseh and was a core group member in 7 Habits was Josh. Josh was a veteran of the war and did a few tours over in Iraq. He was very smart and was business savvy. When we would put together a program or alter one to fit the schedules of the prison, Josh was the man to get it done with ease. He thought with the mind of taking it apart and rebuilding it piece by piece, and not with emotions. I had the most respect for Josh, not only as a friend but also as a man that put his life on the line for my freedom. Our veterans of these wars need to be recognized for their service and their commitment to keeping our country safe.

As mentors in the substance abuse unit at OCC, we put together a good class, and the Psychology of Incarceration was Keys and Josh's baby. They were good teaching it, and Rueski was really insightful and educated in the material. I liked the class and helped quite a bit, but in the end, I stepped back because the room they had us in was small, and those three men didn't need my help. The class was a success at both prisons. Like all good things, it had to come to an end. Mr. Bless moved on, and his replacement closed shop on the class being taught in SAU.

Speaks from the Heart

I was asked to participate in a program that met once a month and had five inmates meet with five to seven men from the Sarpy County Diversion Program. The idea was to have them share their story of why they were in the program and what crime or crimes they had committed to be put in the program. The diversion program is a light sentence instead of going to prison, but if they screw up the program, the judge can sentence them to prison time. The probation officer that brought the men in was a lady called April, and she and I hit it off in a way that was a professional match. When I would pick up on someone that was not being honest, I would call them on it. Then April would pull the covers off them and work them until they got down to the facts of their troubles.

Men living within the prison system should have the responsibility to tell them what to expect if they come to prison. I was brutally honest. I did this for about eight months in a row. I was offered a permanent spot for the monthly meeting. One day, April told me as soon as I was paroled to look her up at the probation office for a job helping men deal with their addictions. I knew that I had a knack for it, and I had a lot of men approaching me in hopes that I would sponsor them in their recovery. I look at it in a sense that I am walking my walk, and my walk matched my talk. I believe that in prison and in the world that lies outside of these fences, it means a lot to see someone that is not full of duplicities in their actions. In prison, a man is known by his actions and his word; they both better match. If not, he is labeled, and not in a good way.

I love being in OCC and helping people. Word was out on how I was telling my story to the diversion program and in the SAU. This helped people take notice that I was on the up-and-up in all my dealings. I was called to the unit manager's office, and he asked if I would be interested in talking with the high school and college students that visited the prison on tours. I was told that word on the street was that I did great job at Tecumseh, and I had an impact on the kids when I told my story. My story had substance. I shared the lessons that I had learned with the students. I accepted the offer to speak to the tours. I did it at Tecumseh and liked it, so I committed to doing it here at OCC.

One thing I always tell the kids is how I found the meaning of the ripple effect. I filled them in on who I was and what had happened in my life that led me to commit crimes. I talked about my prison experiences. Then I would tell them how I tried to escape and how I hurt a guard. When I talk about it, I choke up a little every time. They are shocked when I tell them what I did, how much time I received for it, and how much time I spent in segregation. I love the questions that they ask me. It gives me a chance to talk to them about forgiveness. I always talk about the ripple effect of my choices and who was caused pain and grief. Especially my victim and his family. This gets very personal, and I wouldn't have it any other way.

I also teach them the meaning of a true apology. I went through life saying that I was sorry for this or that. But I only did this when I was caught. I don't remember all the times I was high and broke instead of staying at home and paying my bills, only to say I was sorry. And when the weekend was upon me, I was out and at it again. Shallow apologies or any apology for that matter had no meaning. I went through life that way.

When I apologized to Mr. F, I knew that I would have to change my behavior. I knew that I would never repeat that action again, and I would take the lessons that I had learned and share them with others. *To me, this was a true apology, a heartfelt down-to-the-soul I am sorry.* This was the first of many apologies that were from my heart. It is very important to me to have a platform for sharing the importance of forgiveness and also the need for victim-oriented programming within the prison system.

I had an opportunity to speak to the Criminal Justice class from the University of Omaha, and the professor was none other than former director of the Department of Corrections, Mr. Robert Houston. I walked into the room, and it was filled with about thirty students. The warden and her staff were in attendance too. Mr. Houston walked up to me and gave me a hug then introduced me to his students. I knew I had come a long way, and to have the chance to be part of the solution and not the problem was a big deal for me. This was the future of the criminal system that I was talking to, the future wardens, prosecutors, judges, and law enforcement. I have spoken to more than a few college classes, and I always feel that I have made a difference in some way, shape, or form.

I was asked to give my testimony to the population at a Christian revival that was being held in the commons area of the prison. I took the podium and told my story to about 150 inmates that were in attendance. I spoke about how God changed my life. To me, that was the hardest speech I had done. I bared my soul to a bunch of killers, rapist, burglars, petty thieves, and men who have committed some terrible crimes. I was given a standing applause when I was finished speaking. To me, that was the greatest feeling of all. I talked about my life and my beliefs. I knew I could help someone else open their heart and find God as I had done. I was focusing on some of the men who were caught up in the hate groups. I showed them that I stood strong in my beliefs and that I would not succumb to the social mirror. I am no Bible thumper. I believe in God and will share that with anyone who wants to know.

One thing about sharing your life with the whole prison population is that they watch every move you make, and if you are phony, you will be put on blast. I was a walking testimony, and my walk matched my talk. In prison, there are so many phony and duplicitous people whose words are no good. To be a man of integrity and have your word is huge in this environment. In prison, a man is known by his word, and that is all a man has in this crazy dark world that exists behind the razor wire. If your word is no good, then more than likely, you are no good. The men that I hung out with are cut from the same cloth. We talk recovery, we talk forgiveness, we are about helping the next man, and we are about doing the right things in life.

Change your core beliefs, your value system, and then your thinking will change. That is what the 7 Habits is all about, and those habits or principles are also found in scripture. They are found in philosophy books and in all types of self-help books as well.

I learned it, and so have the men that I hang out with. I believe that iron sharpens iron, and in here, you are judged by the company you keep. Birds of a feather flock together, as they say. To be a positive role model and leader is very gratifying in this negative environment. To overcome the odds, to break the prison code, and to be a trailblazer of a movement that is about reform and transformation is something that I never thought I would be involved with.

What a View

The boss said, "Tom, get that ladder and come with me and the maintenance worker. We are going over to housing unit two. We have to climb up to the roof and try to find a leak. Be careful because the ice and snow is really deep up there."

I couldn't believe it. It had been less than two years since I had been in OCC, and I was being trusted to climb up forty some feet to the roof. I knew the boss wanted me to get the experience of seeing the river. I wondered how many men got the opportunity to be on top of a roof in prison and be up there legitimately. I climbed the ladder, and we found the leak. The view was beautiful. I could see the old railroad bridge and the tree line up and down the Missouri River. I felt alive and had a grin on my face. The boss said that I would never be able to wash off.

It wasn't but a few months after the roof experience when I was asked to help the boss walk around the perimeter fence and put zip ties around the sensor wire. It was to stop the alarm from going off every time the wind blew hard. Here I was, making the prison more secure. I thought, *Hell, twenty-five years ago, I was trying to get through a fence like that*. Life had changed for me, and I was being trusted. That gave me a sense of accomplishment. It meant that all my hard work was being noticed. I was getting rewarded in a way that was satisfying to the soul.

We had numerous graduation ceremonies for the 7 Habits classes here at OCC. We also had a guest speaker for each graduation. When Mr. Larry Wayne was our guest speaker, he showed up with Director Kinney. After the graduation, Mr. Kinney walked up to me and shook my hand. He said, "Tom, you are doing a great job, and I want you to know that there are a lot of people in the Department of Corrections that are inspired by you. You are an inspiration to both inmates and the administration." I stood there with tears running down my cheeks and had a hard time talking. I thanked him and just nodded as he spoke about how the 7 Habits was helping change the culture within the prison system. I think about that day quite often. I knew that I was making a difference, not only within my own life but the life of others.

I was saddened by the news of an inmate whom I spent some time with back in 2009 when we both were in segregation. When he was released, he killed some innocent people in Omaha. It raised a firestorm within the prison system. This guy did about five years in segregation. He did his time day for day. Which means his time was up and the prison could not hold him any longer. The public brought up the issue of inmates being released without supervision. The man did his time and was released from segregation to the streets, then killed three people.

The legislators did their investigations, and someone had to pay the price. It was a witch's hunt, and there needed to be scapegoats. The director and the deputy director were forced into retirement or be fired. I was pissed. These men were good men and were helping incarcerated men change their lives. They were responsible for me being in OCC, and they were the driving force behind the 7 Habits on the Inside program. I wrote a letter to the inspector general and asked him why they were blaming segregation for the reason this inmate had killed three people. I explained to him that the segregation unit did not create the insanity; the insanity was already there. If the segregation unit created that, then the segregation unit also created me. I was doing positive things with my life. I was also making positive choices. This man did five years in segregation while I did thirteen years. How can you justify that statement? I never did get an answer to my inquiries. Typical for the bureaucrats.

I was called up to the captain's office one day during work. He asked me to be in the first MRT class. MRT stands for Moral Reconation Therapy. I said okay. He explained to me that I was a big influence in getting men into the 7 Habits classes. He wanted to use me in MRT in hopes of spreading the news that it was a good program and help it get off the ground. I thought that the MRT was just like 7 Habits, but just not as deep. I voiced my opinion that MRT should be a precursor to 7 Habits because they go hand in hand. I liked the course and found out later that judges were sentencing people to MRT in the county courts.

In my first class, I said that I was a victim of abuse from my dad. This was a no-no according to the rules. Captain P and I had a disagreement that turned into me telling him that he had me in the MRT to toot his horn and to put a feather in his cap. This was the wrong thing to say. He lit into me and had me stay after class. He explained to me why he was facilitating MRT, why he believed in the program, and why he wanted me in it. I had a newfound respect for the captain after that. I learned that the captain did care and wanted me to succeed in life. I finished the class. I became a facilitator's aide in assisting the captain in his class. I helped a countless number of men understand MRT. I had a front row seat in watching these men change their lives and make smarter choices. I was also asked to assist two other facilitators with their MRT classes. I proudly accepted the offer. I became a good fit with the program, and I understand its philosophy.

I believe that when a man takes a look at his life, especially from childhood, he sees that he could have made better choices. He realizes he is not a victim but an owner of his choices. Only then can he take ownership of his life. The man must also want to change. I see many men take these programs because the parole board looked highly upon some of these such as MRT. The only thing that I see as a positive when these men take a program thinking they can persuade the board to give them parole is that they open themselves up to be influenced in a positive manner. I have seen a lot of men that were on game when they came into MRT and leave with a new attitude about how they conduct themselves. I sit in these rooms with the sole purpose of planting seeds of change. I cannot force an individual to see life as I see it, but I can open up his mind by giving him a new paradigm to see through.

11

Silver Linings

I was behind the tiller tilling the garden when it jumped on me. I hung on for dear life. I felt the pop in my right knee. I knew it was not good, and I probably tore my ACL again. I limped around for a while until it quit hurting. I knew that my days in grounds and working in the garden was coming to an end. It was getting harder to lift any weight and carry anything without my knee hurting or buckling on me.

I found out that there was an opening in education, and I went up to talk to Mrs. Z and Mrs. Sturm, who are the teachers. I was hired right away. Mrs. Sturm is also a facilitator for the 7 Habits on the Inside and knows my work ethic. Mrs. Z was my unit manager back in Tecumseh and was aware of my changes.

I did not want to change jobs, but I knew that I wouldn't last long in the garden and working for grounds with a bum knee. My back started hurting again. I was diagnosed with spinal stenosis back in the nineties, and every now and then, it would start to make my legs go numb when I walked. I knew I would miss driving the small tractor and the Z-Trak. Working outside would be dearly missed. I love being outside because of all the segregation time I did. I did thirteen years without the sun shining on my skin for more than an hour a day. I was cooped up twenty-three hours a day for all those years, and the last place I wanted to be was in a cell or inside a building. I was a little bummed about the inside job, but I weighed the pros and cons for taking or not taking the job. It was a no-brainer. I was about to be a teacher's aide.

I do not know how to type or how to use a computer. Being locked up for thirty years, I knew nothing about computers. They were not widely on the market in the mid-eighties, nor were they a household item. Working in education would give me the opportunities to not only learn to how to type but also take classes with Metro Community College. I was about to learn how to operate a computer. I would eventually take a class that gave me the basic skills of using Word, Excel, and PowerPoint.

When I returned to the housing unit from work, I was summoned to the SAU supervisor's office. She wanted me to assist one of her new counselors in starting up a new small group within the program. I said that I would be more than happy to assist him. I entered the endeavor with a good attitude and had the men opening up and talking about their trust issues. In prison, there is still this outlook where most men do not want to show any emotions or they will look weak in front of their peers. We had a good group for a while, but the counselor was new and wanted to do it his way. He started to alienate the men. I tried to help, but I was eventually pushed out.

I had a talk with the supervisor, and she came off real snotty toward me, and then said that I needed to seek forgiveness and some people would never give me a chance in life. I took it as disrespectful and knew that the real reason behind all the attitudes with her and her assistants was the fact that most of her clients in the program were seeking the mentor's advice and not their counselors.

I was helping these men with their first three steps in the recovery program, and a few asked me to be their sponsor. They would seek my advice and then tell their one-on-one counselor that I had already helped them. This caused a huge conflict. I ended up being pushed out of the very program that I helped start. I was the only one left from the original men that built the mentor program in OCC.

I was called back to the unit one day and was told to pack my property. I was being moved to another unit. It was bittersweet, but I was glad to be out of there. I believe I was burning out and needed a break from the programming mindset. I was clean and sober and working a program. The in-house treatment mindset was starting get to me in the end. I moved. I was put into a room with some youngsters who were living in active addiction. I knew that I would not be residing in that cell very long. I started to look for a cell in another unit. The other units had two-man cells. It wasn't long before a cell opened up in Unit 2. I moved into it and took Big Stacy with me.

Big Stacy and I went way back. This was like his fourth time back in prison. It is a good feeling living with a person that is clean, and you can trust him with your property. We were both working a recovery program, so it was a no-brainer to move him into the cell. I got him a job on the bucket crew, picking up trash and cutting grass. I worked in education, so when I was gone, he would be in the cell cooking candy balls. When I was in the cell, he would be out on the yard, so the arrangement worked out really well.

Rising above Your Circumstances

I was asked to be part of a workshop. Diane from MCC was putting it together. The workshop was called *Living above Your Circumstances*. The workshop dealt with changing while still inside the fences and not falling into the daily bull that went on within the prison. It was such a success that we had to add two more sessions to fit all the inmates that were interested in it. The event was held in the education classroom, and the room was full. It was a roundtable discussion with about thirty inmates and ten ex-cons from the street in attendance.

One thing about prison is you learn right away that around 90 percent of the inmates are full of crap. As I will always express, in prison, you can be anyone you want to be. I have met men who said they were gunrunners but ended up being petty thieves. Then there was the man that was a pimp and had a stable full of women. In reality, he was a drunk doing time for his tenth DUI. I always liked the guy who would tell you that he sold so much dope that he owned expensive cars, boats, motorcycles, and houses. Then he would ask you for a spoonful of coffee. These men are what the system is full of. It is not the norm to practice integrity and just be you. Many of men say they were set up and it is someone else's fault that they are locked up. So to be surrounded by men and women who were themselves and wanted something better for their lives instead of the con games that are in prison was refreshing, to say the least.

I realized that these men and women who are living on the other side of the fences are doing well but are not without struggle. They made a choice to live above the circumstances that surrounded them and made a change in their lives while still behind the wire. Here they are, coming back inside to show the men on the inside that they can make it on the outside. I know it was hard for some of them to walk back through those doors and here the clang as they shut behind them. They expressed that in the workshop. The thing that impressed me was that they were honest on how hard it was to succeed when they were released from prison. They talked about what they did to get through it so that when the next man walked out those doors, they would know what to expect. They also talked about starting their change while still in prison so they would be able to rise above the challenges that were ahead of them.

The prison code is one thing that you learn when you come into prison. You sit back and you watch what the men do and not do. I learned that you do not walk and talk to a guard while alone. You have to have someone with you when you talk to any authority figure. That is an example of a code or the norm in prison. *Keep your mouth shut, mind your own business, and do your own time are parts of that prison code.*

I ask the men who are in every 7 Habits class if they know what breaking the prison code is. The first thing they say is that it sounds like snitching. It never fails. There is always one person in the class and usually more than one to say that. I love telling them if a man makes the right choices in his life and is no longer allowing the social mirror dictate his choices, he can break that code. It isn't a bad thing to stand up and take control of your life. I used myself as an example. I explain how I can stand up in front of them in the 7 Habits class, and helping the facilitators teach the course is all about breaking that code. I am working with guards, unit managers, unit administrators, teachers, and a deputy director. How can a convict work with prison officials and still have good standing with the prison population? I then give them the answer. I am accountable for my own actions. I do not cower to the pressure from my peers. I call it breaking the social mirror. I am making a difference by being a core group member and showing these men that if I can change my life, they have no excuse for not changing theirs.

I love breaking it down and explaining how I see the formula for change. There are a lot of men who have violated their parole when they were released. They were locked up again for a new crime. I was that man who was released on parole, only to fall back into the same behavior that led to my incarceration in the first place. The first thing that I had to change was my value system. I value honesty today. In the past, I did not value it at all. On the scale of high and low, I was on one side or the other when it came to a value system.

I Am Grateful to You, Dr. Covey

Dr. Covey talks about adding value to principles. Honesty today is the same as honesty was one thousand years ago in China. Honesty is a principle that will never change. I have honesty, accountability, responsibility, etc. The thing with value is, I can add to it or take away from it.

For most of my life, I had a low value of accountability. I blamed everyone else for my problems. I even blamed the judge who sentenced me for my lengthy incarceration. I didn't look at the fact that I had broken the law to get arrested and sentenced to begin with. Once I changed my value system, I realized that my thinking had changed. Dr. Covey said that when you change your value system, you're thinking changes, and then your behavior changes. Once your behavior changes, the results of those actions or the consequences of your actions change.

I saw how the ripple effect worked in my life. I had changed by being responsible for my own life first. Then after evaluating my life, especially the way I perceived the world, I knew that I wanted to change. I envisioned how I wanted my life to be when I turned eighty years old. What do I want my children to say about me when

I am eighty? What kind of father did I want to be? I am talking about the right here and now and not the past thirty years of incarceration. From today forward was my new attitude. What kind of husband do I want my wife to say I was if I was to marry again? What kind of best friend am I? What would my boss say about me as a worker? These are the things that I had learned in 7 Habits class and applied to my life. All I needed was a plan to make it happen. I knew what kind of man I wanted to become, and it would be hard, but I had the testicular fortitude to get it done.

When I speak to the tours, I tell the students that I am a recovering addict. Every day that I wake up, I envision myself laying my head upon my pillow that night clean and sober. Then I plan my day accordingly so that I can accomplish that goal. I had changed my value system. I had learned that I have always had some principles in my core beliefs, but I did not value them very much. Now that I knew who I wanted to be, I now knew what I needed to change value wise. I changed my core values, and my thinking changed. I was now focused on being that best friend and that good father who was there for his children. All my actions were a result of my thinking.

I have a mission statement that reads, "I am accountable for all my actions, responsible for all my decisions, and I will forgive others as I have so richly been forgiven. Then I will take all the lessons that I have learned in my life and share them with others. I value accountability, responsibility, and forgiveness today. These are the things that I did not give much value to my whole life. The things that kept me screwed up are the things that I had to change in my life and go in the opposite direction."

How simple it sounded when Dr. Covey talked about it. As I look back at all I have accomplished in my life, it was because of his simple formula. Change your core values, you change your thinking. Change your thinking, you change your attitude and behavior. Change your attitude and behavior, you change the consequences of those behaviors. *The good old rule of cause and effect.* You do righteous acts, and then you should have righteous results. You do unmoral acts, then the results should be unrighteous.

If my core value system revolves around self-gratification (addiction), then I will be thinking about pleasing that or feeding that beast until I am gratified. This means I will be chasing my tail all day long until I am sated. My actions will result in robbing some establishment or committing a burglary or a petty theft, whatever it takes to get money. The end result will be jail, prison, or, maybe even death.

Here I am, applying a core value system that is centered in valuing the principles that are in my mission statement. The end result is about helping people see what I saw. I teach them that if you can change your thinking and apply values to your life, then you are not likely to return to the same lifestyle that existed in before you were locked up. As those who came before me had taught me how they changed their life. They explained to me what they did to accomplish it. They took all the excuses away from me. I have no excuse for not succeeding. If they can do it, then there is no reason that I can't.

I take all the excuses away from all the men that I share my story with and all those who know about the changes I had made in my life. I am the infamous violent man who has many violent robberies on his record. I tried to escape. I hurt a guard, which led to thirteen years of segregation time. I served more than thirty years in prison, most of it being a negative influence in a negative environment. I finally turned my life around. There are no excuses for anyone in the prison system to not change. I have also learned that a person has to have that urge to change. *They must want to change profoundly within the very depths of their being.*

When has a person reached rock bottom? Most people want to change when they hit rock bottom. I thought that I had hit bottom when I went to prison the first time. I was paroled, and then I dug the bottom even deeper. I committed more robberies and extended my prison sentence. I didn't stop there. I tried to escape and hurt a guard. I was placed in a segregation cell for the next thirteen years. Two decades later, I learned that I had not changed my core value system. This was why the bottom had kept dropping out from under me. I believe rock bottom is *when a person decides to quit digging.* Once you decide to quit digging, you will find a way to climb up and out of whatever prison that you have made for yourself.

I've had a lot of people ask me when I was going to write a book. I had a sergeant ask me back in Tecumseh. He would say, "Hey, Fleming, you working on that book yet? You need to write a book, man. You have been through some crap and changed. You need to tell folks about it." I even had an ombudsman ask me if I had planned to write a book. I kept thinking that no one wanted to hear what I have to say or read about my life. Then I started thinking about it. I thought about all the books that I had read over the years. It dawned on me that most of the men who wrote books about their prison life end up glorifying the prison code.

I have read some righteous books about change from a few prisoners. I had the opportunity to read *My Shadow Runs Fast* by Bill Sands. This book was about a formula for change and was the influence for a group he founded in prison called The 7th Step Foundation. This group was big in Kansas and spread to Washington State, and eventually to Nebraska. I believe it is still active in the Nebraska prison system as a self-help club.

Encouragement from Wally

Then there was *The Upside of Fear* and *The Power of Consistency* by Weldon Long. Weldon Long is a man who served time in the Colorado prison system and studied *The 7 Habits of Highly Effective People* by Dr. Covey. I read Wally's books and learned that he uses a formula that consists of your thinking controlling your emotions. Your emotions control your actions. Your actions control the results of your choices. He talks about focus, emotional commitment, actions, and responsibility in his book called *The Upside OF Fear*.

There was one inmate that also read his books and was so impressed that he started a writing campaign to get Mr. Weldon Long to come to OCC to talk to the inmates about his successes and how he accomplished them. It took months before it was all set for Mr. Long to come to Omaha. Mrs. Sturm worked hard setting it all up, and I know the men who were lucky enough to hear Mr. Long speak were grateful for her efforts. Mr. Long ended up speaking twice. There were a so many men who wanted to hear him talk. We ended up having two sessions.

I sat there and listened to Wally talk about his change and his meeting Dr. Covey. Then he spoke about the impact that the *7 Habits* book had made in his life. I was very impressed. I told Wally that I wanted to write a book, and he encouraged me to do so. He also gave me a few tips to get started. I hear these men tell their stories, and I look at my story. It is hard not to compare how a man did his time, how much time he served, or how much violence there was. It always should end in how much change he did. We all are a result of a broken core value system. It seems to be the common thread of the incarcerated.

A lot of men and women incarcerated have been conditioned at a young age to believe that they are not good enough or that they will never amount to anything. A lot of us were subjected to physical or sexual abuse at a young age. Some of us were influenced by our peers or introduced to drugs and alcohol. Conditioning is something that is hard to break because it is so deeply embedded in our value system.

When I realized that I had made a wreck out of my life, I knew that I could change because of people like, Bill Sands and Weldon Long. They had the testicular fortitude to change their lives and to write about it. They shared the details of their lives with me. They took the excuses away from me, just as I take away the excuses from those I come in contact with. They read a lot of influential literature by the likes of Dr. Stephen R. Covey, Napoleon Hill, Albert Einstein, Buddha, Victor Frankl, Goethe, Emerson, and countless other classics and self-help books.

One of things that Weldon Long said that moved me was how *our expectations are the ceiling of our results*. In other words, if I only expect to get to the moon, then I will never get beyond the moon. Why limit yourself, he says. I agree and thought that it was a profound saying, and it stuck with me.

I do not want to get out of prison and flip burgers for the rest of my life. I want to do something great with my life. I want to help others overcome their weaknesses. I see myself working with people who have addictions and are in trouble with the law. I see myself helping them change their paradigms and their thinking.

I also took Weldon's advice and put up a vision board in my cell. It consists of a picture of a new house by a lake and also a picture of the Harley I want to own. I even put up a $ sign of $60,000. That is how much I want to make a year. I know that this is a vision that will be reality one day. I will have these things in my life. I think big, therefore my attitude and behavior started to match my thinking. Before long, the results of those actions, the cause and effect, was evident. I was seeing huge changes in my life that were positive.

12

Giving Back

I knew that I had made a 180 degree turn when I was approached by Corporal Hanson, who is the training officer here at OCC. He asked me if I would come into the training room and tell the new hires my story, then answer questions like I did with the tours. I was shocked. Here I was, the man who was used in the departments training sessions in a negative way for years. The training staff had portions of the 1991 escape attempt recorded. They were using the footage to show the new hires just how dangerous the prison can be. They used me in a negative manner for years. I had new officers walk by me and say, "Shake down, Fleming." I was wondering how this guy knew my name. This happened frequently.

One day, two caseworkers were standing in the commons area of the education department. They told me that they saw me on a video. It showed me trying to commandeer the trash truck. This occurred when they were in training, and they also told me that the training officer talked about me in a negative manner. So to be used in the training room with the new hires in a positive manner was fulfilling, to say the least. I feel that I am not only being trusted, but the administration trusts me with the community's children when I speak to them during tours. And now I am being trusted with the new prison guards when I speak to them in the training room.

I think back to the first time I used empathy but did not realize that it was empathy at the time. When I met with Mr. F during the Victim Offender Dialogue Program, he was telling me about everything that he went through because of me. As I sat there listening to him, I tried putting myself in his shoes. I tried to understand exactly what it was that he went through. It wasn't until I discovered habit five in the 7 Habits class, when one of the facilitators explained what empathy was. It hit me like a ton of bricks. I had a flashback to the day that I met with Mr. F, and the word *empathy* took on a deep and personal meaning to me.

I had a friend that was in a wheelchair, and he decided to enroll in the MRT. He had rough time writing and talking. He also had bad eyes, so it was hard for him to do the work that was required for the class. I talked to the facilitator, and she allowed John to work on the lessons with my assistance. It was one-on-one tutoring sessions. When John completed each step, he would then sit in on the classes with the rest of the men and give his advice. This helped John feel like he was a part of the class and still useful in a way. I never thought that I would be the man who helped others in a way that was so private yet so profound. No one knew that I was helping John but John and the facilitator. I took the lessons that I learned in 7 Habits and applied them with John. I had discovered that it was empathy that I was using to make those choices in my life, choices like helping those less fortunate than I.

My friend Kenny Ferndog showed up at OCC. He just came from the Lincoln D&E Center. He said he violated parole again. He had to do another year or so before the board would give him another shot at parole. Back in 2007, Kenny was at Tecumseh with me, and I did not know who he was until one of my guys said that this youngster from south Omaha had some trouble with one of the cliques. I introduced myself to him, and he already knew who I was. I told him since he was from south Omaha and I heard that he was good people that I would get the clique off his back. I straightened it out with the clique dudes, and Kenny did not have any problems after that. I had a soft spot for these kids out of my neighborhood, and I tried to make their time easier than it was by taking them under my wing. I tried to teach them to be the solution in their neighborhood instead of the problem. Kids like Kenny stole from their own backyard to fuel their addictions. I try to change their paradigm to let them see the situation from my eyes. I was proud of Kenny when he told me that he knew how he went wrong and put together a plan to change some things in his life. He didn't make the same bad choices again. It is rewarding when these kids discover that they have choices and recognize that it is their choices that cause their fall from society.

I've seen men who violated their parole over and over, like my bro Big Sean. You think they have it all figured out, then they come back again. One thing they always do is tell me how the streets are, and then they glorify the dope game. I believe that unless a man totally removes himself from the source, he will relapse into that default setting that he has been conditioned to rely upon. When times get bad, they go back to using. It is easier than facing the problem and finding a solution to it. The fear of the unknown and failure is huge on the psyche too. I think that when we go back to what we know, it is failure in itself. What was it that Einstein said? I believe he said, "If a person does the same thing over and over again expecting different results, that thinking is insanity." The prison system is full of men who continue to live in that state of mind, and it is a shame. To be part of the solution is rewarding in itself. I feel that the system should address these issues, and I have tried to voice my opinion, but the system does not listen to the inmate when it comes to facing the problems of a broken system.

Those That Pave the Way

I want to take a minute and talk about some of the men that I have known over the years who have made it successfully on parole. I have a friend who is known by the name of Pork Chop. Pork Chop did a few years in the segregation unit while he was incarcerated. He did about ten years in prison before he was paroled. This brother had six years to do on parole. I am here to tell you that this man takes away all the excuses from anyone that is on parole and violates. There is no reason that a man should violate parole if he is living his life correctly in line with the rules and obeying the laws. Pork Chop was just released from parole. This man worked hard from the time he hit the work release center to the time he was put on parole. He saved his money and ended up running a salvage yard. The last I heard, he was part owner of the company. This gives me the incentive to succeed. My friend Pork Chop has taken all the excuses away from any man on parole. Men like Pork Chop, Keys, Rue, Josh, Butch, and countless others are excellent examples of men who value their freedom. They changed their core value system. These men have changed their thinking; therefore, they have changed their behavior.

The men that come into prison tell me about all the changes that are going on in society, in my old neighborhood, and it boggles my mind. They have cars that talk to you and park themselves. This blows my mind! I think a lot about my transition back into society, and I wonder if I will adjust to all the changes that have happened over the past three decades. Thirty years is a long time to be separated from society.

I think about dating again, and I wouldn't know if a woman was hitting on me or not. I laugh because she could smile at me and I would think she wanted me, but in reality, she was just being polite. I have a lot of insecurities about leaving the world that I have thrived in for over half of my life. I ask myself if I can get a job. Who will hire an ex-con who just did over thirty years behind the razor wire? Will I fit in, and where will I fit in at? I wonder if I am overthinking these things sometimes, but I can't help it. One of my fears is entering a supermarket and standing in an aisle looking at bars of soap and being stuck because I am too overwhelmed by all the choices. In prison, there are only three brands to choose from. I know when I think about these things, I do not let it consume my thoughts.

I've seen men who let their worries overtake their senses to the point that they throw it all away. I learned from Dr. Covey that I have a circle of concern and a circle of influence. I call it my circle of concern and my circle of no concern. What can I do about it? And if I can't, then leave it alone. Many of men trip on their family, and these are legitimate concerns. However, if your girlfriend doesn't answer the phone when you call, do you walk around with your head down, worried that she is cheating on you? I see it all the time, and it is a sad thing to watch.

Men trip on what their children are doing when they know they have two more years to do before they get out. Again, a legitimate concern, but should it consume your thoughts to the point that you are yelling at your wife, telling her she is a terrible mother? I have no control of the situation when my girlfriend is cheating on me while I sit in prison. I put myself in this situation, and I only have control of my own choices. I do not control anything or anyone outside my current situation. This is one of the hardest lessons to teach a man that is doing time. I use my life as an example.

My dear elderly mother is closing in on eighty years old, and my father is in his eighties. Mom has bad legs and had to go to the hospital because she couldn't walk or even get out of bed. She was put in a rehabilitation center and has been there for months. I am worried as a son should be, but I do not have any control over the situation. I do not let it consume me to the point that it is all that I think about. I learned this in 7 Habits and am very grateful that I can separate what I control and what I do not have control over. There was a time that I knew my former wife Juki was cheating on me, and I let it consume my thoughts to the point that I dived deeper into addiction. I was taking all my pain out on my friends and family.

MRT really points this out, when the student has to write his worries, wants, and needs down on paper and talk about it. I always ask the student if he has control over that worry, and he says no. This is when I ask him why he is worried about it then. What it does is opens his mind to a new paradigm. He assesses the things that he is worried about and consumed by. He looks at it in a new light. One of the things that I have expressed to the Department of Corrections is that once a man has taken MRT, he should be placed in the 7 Habits from the Inside Program. It is a one-two punch that opens up the mind from the depths of his core values. A few of the facilitators have agreed, and a few of the administrators have agreed, but that is as far as it has gone. One day, I will be in the position to bring about change within the prison system. This has been put on my heart.

What would the broken man do? I know! He would forge his own tools, nuts, and bolts and repair his broken self. Then broken man would fix the broken system. Look out, broken world!

I learned over the years that I was broken. I had told my mother I was changing and doing well, but I was still in the segregation unit and getting into trouble. I couldn't figure out why she never believed me. When I had stopped talking about changing and started to change from the inside out, the consequences of my actions changed. When I had taken the semester class with Peru State College, I sent Mom the certificate I received. When I completed the SAU program, I sent Mom the certificate. When I was interviewed for the story in the local newspaper, I sent Mom a copy of the article. These things added up. It was no longer me blowing smoke. *I was actually sending the results of my actions to her, and it was up to her to decide if it was a deposit or not in her emotional bank account.* When I was transferred to Omaha from Tecumseh, it was all the proof that any of my family needed to realize that I was changing. I was no longer that man who walked out of their lives and into decades of separation. It was that true apology in action. I had changed my behavior and did not repeat those mistakes. I was sharing these lessons that I have learned with others. There is no better feeling than gaining the trust of those that are dear to our heart and those that you have hurt by your bad choices in life.

I looked up from my desk, and there stood Corporal K with two teenagers standing beside her. She introduced me to them then told me they were her children, and she was giving them a tour of where she worked. Then she asked me to tell them my story and answer their questions. I told them all about me and the choices I had made. I told them how I turned a three- to seven-year sentence into a forty-four to 117 year prison sentence. They had some great questions as most of the high school students usually do. When they left, I sat there in awe of the situation that had just happened.

Here I was at OCC, sitting in the education department assisting men get their GED, and I had a guard bring her kids in to see me and have me talk to them. What a heartwarming experience I had just been through. I thought about that day for weeks and tried to make sense out of it. I came to the conclusion that this was the consequences of my actions of the past ten years. I had been making deposits in the trust department and did not realize that everyone that had contact with me was prone to being caught up in the ripple effect of my positive actions. I was doing the right things and sharing them with others, I chalk it up to the emotional bank account that 7 Habits teaches. I spoke with the tours, and this particular corporal heard me talk and share my story several times. She has also watched my behavior on the yard. I had made an impact on some level for her to trust me to speak with her children.

Ripples That Hurt

I think about the ripple effect that continues to expand, even after all these years. I tossed that pebble into the waters of life over thirty years ago. My children are still living in the consequences of my actions. My daughter, Holly, was raised without a father in her life. She did not have her father there to protect her when the world got tough. I think about that all the time; I have apologized to my children many of times for my not being there in their lives as a dad and a father. My daughter is fighting addiction in her life as I write this book, and she has lost her children temporally as a result of her addictions. My youngest son, Thomas Jr., who was raised by same mother as Holly, has also fought the beast of addiction. I was not there for him when the world got rough. I was told by both of my youngest children that they had a terrible childhood. Their mother was moving men in and out of their house and had a drinking problem herself. I do not blame Juki for everything those children were subjected to. I did blame myself for not being that role model they needed so desperately in their lives.

My oldest son, Joe, was shuffled around as a child. Juki said she could not handle him, and I took him to my mother's home to be raised. My parents couldn't handle him, so my youngest sister took him in. It did not last long, and he was placed into the Home for Boys. Part of that ripple effect was that I met a good person who would become a great friend. Bill Auxier is his name.

As Joe grew up without that positive father figure in his life, he turned to drugs and fell deep into addiction. This was the son who was bringing me drugs while I was in segregation. I was a bad role model to my children, and they were holding me in high esteem for the wrong reasons as they grew up. I was that gangster figure they thought was cool. In reality, I was a broken man that had messed my life up and theirs. That ripple effect lasts a lifetime. Now my son is serving a twenty-year sentence for manslaughter, which was drug related. I taught him to smuggle drugs into prison for me, and he did time for transporting dope. He went deeper and deeper into the criminal thinking and behavior, just as I had done.

Today I teach my children that a man can change his life. I also teach them the philosophy behind cause and effect. I use my own life and theirs as a teaching tool. I found out that even though I am not home with them, I can be a positive influence in their lives. I share with them the important things like empathic listening techniques and the importance of having goals. When they tell me how they are using those things that I teach them, I smile and hope they are not blowing smoke up my rear as I did with my parents. I always think of that good old saying that I use: *time will either prove you or expose you.*

I call my grandchildren a couple of times a week and talk to them. I love planting seeds in my conversations. I will ask them if they said anything that was hurtful to anyone that day. Then I will talk about how they felt when someone said things that hurt them. I love teaching them about empathy, and I pray that they put these things into use one day. I am being a positive influence in their lives in the hopes that there is a ripple effect that brings about positive consequences in their lives.

Inspiration from Larry Wayne

I received letters from Former Deputy Director Larry Wayne about every other month, and I got to see him when he visited OCC once a month for Christian Heritage classes. We have formed a friendship that is priceless. Who would have thought that I would be kicking it with former prison officials? I also received a few letters from Former Director Kenney telling me how proud he was of me and the changes that I made in my life. All this stems from the ripple effect of that VOD meeting. This is why I have dedicated my life to be an advocate for that program and one of the reasons that I am writing this book.

I know that for me to tell the world about the power of forgiveness, I would need a big outlet. All of these years, people have been scratching their heads over the fact that I had lived thirteen years in that seven-by-nine-foot cell in the segregation unit and that I have been locked up over thirty years. I still have a sense of humor, and I have a positive outlook about life. This is not normal for someone in my position. I can see why a lot of people wanted me to put my life experiences on paper.

I Have What? Cancer!

I was having problems again with my back. I have spinal stenosis. I was diagnosed with it years ago and was told that I was born with a narrow spinal column. When I walk, my legs would go numb, and pain would shoot down my legs. I could only walk about one to two blocks before I had to stop. I went to the doctor and jumped through all the bureaucratic hoops to get an MRI on my back. I went to the hospital and had the MRI; the results were in about a week later.

The doctor said, "Mr. Fleming, you can sit right here in this chair. It looks like you will be scheduled to see a neurologist for your back. I need to tell you that the MRI has found a spot on your right kidney. It looks like it is renal carcinoma. Mr. Fleming, you have cancer. I have made and appointment with a urologist so we can figure out what we need to do next."

I was informed that I still had to see the neurologist to find out what needed to be done with my back, but the cancer would take precedence over my back. The emotions that flooded my thoughts were overwhelming, to say the least. No one wants to hear that word. That is the word that people dread to have come out of their doctor's mouth. It's a death sentence in most cases. I sat there for a second, and the doc asked me if I was okay. I put on the face that I always put on when faced with a difficult situation and said, "I am cool,

Doc. This isn't going to take me out of the game." I was told that I would see a kidney doctor soon and proceed from there. I smiled and walked out of the building.

I got to the walkway in front of the infirmary and thought I was going to puke. I held my head high, and I thought about how I was going to tell my mom. I can't die while I am in prison. I promised her I would get out and spend time with her before she passed on. I put on the mask that all was going to be okay. Inside, I was a wreck.

The light bulb went off right there and then. I had an MRI on my back because it was causing me pain, and I had a hard time walking. I tore my ACL, which caused the limping and my back to be irritated. This was caused by the tiller jumping on me and tearing my ACL. If it wasn't for the MRI on my back, I would have never known about the cancer. This surely had to be divine intervention. I knew in my heart that this was a gift from God. Kidney cancer is called the silent killer because you do not know you have it until it is too late. I asked to have my back fixed and they discovered cancer. This was not supposed to happen this way. If it wasn't for that MRI, I would be in a bad way. I owe that tiller for tearing my ACL in an odd sort of way. I was told by several people that it was a good way to look at the situation. I knew deep down in the depths of my soul that God had used that tiller to set things in motion.

Silverlinology

I am a self-proclaimed silverlinologist. I have a degree in silverlinology donchano. What is a silverlinologist, you ask? Well, let me tell you what one is. A silverlinologist is a person that finds the silver lining in all the storms that pass through his or her lives. Black clouds bring storms, but there is always a lesson to be learned.

Let us imagine there is this man who has gone to the Fourth of July parade every year since he was a little boy. Now he is thirty years old and is standing on the corner in front of the bookstore where he used to buy comics at. He was excited for the parade to start because for some odd reason, the parade brought him peace and that feeling of innocence, reminding him of when he was a child. As he awaited the start of the parade, he noticed a big black storm cloud in the sky. Before too long, it started to pour rain. He looked around for some shelter from the storm. There was the bookstore right behind him, and he ran inside to get out of the rain.

"Hi," said the woman behind the counter.

Now let's jump forward a year. There stands the man who ran into the bookstore last year to get away from the rainstorm that ruined his parade. He was all excited waiting for the parade to start. He remembered how the storm had changed his life forever, because standing next to him was his new wife, and she was holding their newborn daughter in her arms. If the storm didn't blow into town and ruined the parade last year, he would have not gone into the bookstore and talked to the woman behind the counter. They ended up talking for hours that day, waiting for the storm to pass. They found out that they had a lot in common and that spark of interest was between them. You now know the rest of the story. They ended up together, the beautiful silver lining. Only a self-proclaimed silverlinologist would see the silver lining in that story.

I have to put on my silverlinologist hat and look at the situation at hand. I had an MRI done for my back, and it showed another problem that I wasn't aware of. Now do you believe in silver linings? I want you, the reader, to take a few moments and examine your life. Try to remember a storm that blew through your life. Now seek out the silver lining. Go ahead. Put this book down for a few minutes and be a silverlinologist. Anyone can be a silverlinologist if they can look hard enough and deep enough to seek out the good within all the bad.

I was called up to Captain P's office, and he sat me down to discuss how I was handling the news of my cancer. He told me about how he handled the news of his wife's illness and said he knew what I was going through. This man sincerely cared about me, and I knew this when I went through his MRT class, but I did not know to what extreme. The captain cares about the success of the inmates in his facility. The rarity these days of anyone caring about the welfare of an inmate is few and far in between.

What started as an itch on the left side of my rib cage turned into a rash that was very painful. It was a Saturday evening, and I went to the chow hall to give away my supper. I had no appetite. The pain with this rash was excruciating, to say the least. There stood the captain checking IDs in the chow line. He noticed I was holding my side, and I told him that I thought I had shingles. He laughed and I didn't. He told me to see him after the chow hall closed. I was taken to the medical nurse, and she confirmed that I had shingles. She gave me some medication, and I went back to my cell. I first thanked the captain again, and he said that he was getting used to me breaking down like an old truck.

I went in for my surgery on December 19, 2016, two weeks before my fifty-sixth birthday. I talked to my surgeon, Dr. Kim, right before I went under. She reassured me that it would be a pretty routine operation. I couldn't help to be nervous about it. I kept thinking that the cancer had spread and I was a goner. I woke up in the recovery room, and as soon as I could be moved, I was taken to a regular hospital room. Dr. Kim walked in and told me that the cancer was isolated to just the kidney, and I would be okay. I couldn't wait to call Mom and tell her that I was out of the woods. I called her, and she cried tears of joy. I called my daughter-in-law, Ani, and told her so she could get on the internet and e-mail everyone to give them an update on my progress. I was very relieved to be okay, and I lay there and prayed about it. I just couldn't wrap my mind around the why of it all.

What was supposed to be a week in the hospital ended up being two days. I was operated on a Monday and was back in the prison on Wednesday. I guess my recovery was good. I had gone to the bathroom for the nurses, and I had all my blood work come back normal. My good and remaining kidney was functioning like it was supposed to. I even was cutting back on the narcotics that they were giving me. I didn't want to get strung out on the oxycodones. I was happy to be back in my cell. It seems that I am at ease in the comforts of familiar surroundings.

I was sitting in the captain's MRT class two weeks after my kidney removal, assisting him in the class. After the class, he said that I didn't look very well and asked me what was wrong. I told him that my side hurt and was swollen. He took me right over to medical and had me examined. The next thing I knew, I was rushed to the hospital to be cut open at the same incision site where the doc took out the kidney. I had developed a fever, and fluid had filled the area where I was supposed to be healed. I lay in the hospital as the doctors cut me back open, and I was awake for it. The doctor had his whole hand in my side, and it hurt more than I could handle. I was given a shot in the IV, and it rocked me to the point that I almost puked. The nurse said something about the doc having to make sure there were no more sponges in me. I wonder what that meant. Did they leave a sponge in me to begin with? I was put on a wound vac. This was to help me heal from the inside out. I was sent to the Lincoln Infirmary, which is located in the Lincoln Correctional Center. I was told that the wound vac would heal my wound 50 percent faster than normal. I ended up spending a month in the prison infirmary.

While I was lying in the infirmary, I had a couple of visitors. The door opened up, and there stood a major. This man was a sergeant back in the days when I was a knucklehead. In fact, he was at the prison the day I tried to escape. The major and I talked for over an hour. We talked about the condition that the prison system was in. One thing we spent time on was talking about how I had changed my life after I participated in the VOD with Mr. F. The major had heard I was doing real good and wanted to see exactly where my thoughts were on the future. We even talked about my cancer and the work of the Lord. There was divine intervention in catching the cancer on an MRI that was meant for my back. The major is a Christian, and we talked about the power of God.

The captain had sent my property up to me in the infirmary from OCC. The lieutenant that was on duty one day was on officer that worked the segregation unit back in the nineties. He came by to see if I needed anything. We talked about victim awareness and the need for victim impact classes within the Department of Corrections. We even talked about how his wife donated her kidney to his brother and what she was doing to get back in shape after the surgery.

I was just getting ready for chow when there was a knock on my cell door. Here stood the departments investigator. He was a sergeant back in the early days of my segregation time. He was the one who put the boots to my head. I also saw him when he was a captain at Tecumseh. I greeted him, he talked about how he had heard all the things I was doing in OCC, and he had heard about my cancer and wanted to see me. We had a good talk, and I had forgiven him in my heart years ago. It is good to hear that you are doing well in the eyes of those whom at one time abhorred you. I smiled that day and for a few days afterward. It is so rewarding to the mind and soul to know that your decisions are the right ones, and all the things you have learned and shared with others are making a difference. That is just the ripple effect at work. It took years of change, but the ripples have made it to those who are outside of my daily circles in OCC.

I walked back into the prison here in Omaha. It was good to be back in the open air. It had been thirty days since I had been in the sun and breathing clean air. I missed the sunshine when I did those thirteen years in South Forty. I am the last man that wants to be cooped up in a hospital room or an infirmary cell. Anytime I was in the cell for an extended period, I would get a little edgy. I know I have a lot of things to get used to, but being cooped up isn't one of them.

Teachers Need Praises and Raises Too

I had missed my job in the education center. I love helping the men get their GED. I also missed the teachers. Mrs. Z and Mrs. Sturm are great teachers and great people to be around. I have learned so much from the two of them. The lessons I am learning in dealing with the students are priceless. I also missed the staff from Metro Community College.

I was helping with the Thursday afternoon typing classes, and I was also helping Mrs. Z with the Tuesday afternoon Intro into Microcomputers class. I had excelled so far in that class when I took it. I stayed on to help Mrs. Z teach the class. As a teacher's aide, I have the privilege to get on the computers to get class schedules and sign in sheets ready if need be. I also get to design the upcoming events that are going to be held in the education center. We used to keep the GED inmates' grades on the computer. Now we use the computer to keep track of their registering and there assignments. I get a lot of computer time every week, and I am grateful for that.

Working with the men who are trying to obtain their GED certificate is very rewarding. I had one man whose name is J. Antony come up to me all excited because the math formulas that he was learning finally clicked in his head. I had been working with him and teaching him the proper use of fractions. Learning fractions is very important and necessary in math. I see the smiles on the men's faces when they understand what they are learning and apply it. Grown men taking the initiative to learn and receive their GED and being able to be a part of the process is priceless.

I see Diane from Metro every once in a while when she is in the prison doing some work for Metro. I love the support she and the people that work with her give me. I love it when they tell me that they can't wait until I get over to the work release center so I can go to the reentry center at the college. Metro has a great reentry program. Sharri and Glenn who are with the reentry team come into the prison and help the men learn how to type and utilize the computers here in education. They also take the long termers who have spent more than ten years in prison to the reentry building on campus. They teach them how to use a cell phone and also how to use a tablet. I am blessed to have deep profound conversations with good people like Sharri, Glenn, Marji, Carolyn, Sheila, and Dwayne. Dwayne was released after almost forty years of incarceration. He went to the campus for classes, and once released, he joined the Metro team and loved working in the reentry center. My bro Butch is at the release center, and I was told he is now taking classes at Metro to get his CDL. Butch is going to drive a truck, which was always his dream job. We would sit on the bench while old Frank would feed the birds bread, and we would talk about what we would do when we got out. Butch always said that his dream was to travel the country, especially after serving almost forty years in prison.

Metro Community College is giving men like Butch and I an opportunity to have a career once we get to work release or out of prison. I see so many men take advantage of the classes that they offer. The classes are always full, and there is always someone who does not get into the class they want because of the big turnouts. I like the fact that once you are enrolled in the courses, the people at Metro assist you in getting on a career path. Every person that is in a class will get the first choice to be in the class of their desire for the next semester.

I was told that the video I participated in for MCC had been completed and will be an advertisement for MCC classes. The video will be shown in all the prisons television systems. My son can turn on channel 15 at the state penitentiary and see his pops talking about Metro and the good things that I have learned in taking the courses that they offer. My bro Crow can turn on his TV and go to the inmate channel to see me talking about Metro. This is good for Metro and for my bro to see me after all these years.

Diane told me that there was going to be a big get-together in the commons area, which was right outside the Education Department. There would be MCC bigwigs and state senators there. The director of the Department of Corrections would also be in attendance. She asked me to be one the incarcerated men to speak to the crowd. I said that I would. I feel it is important to tell the audience the importance of getting the opportunity to learn, especially at my age (fifty-six) and after doing this amount of time. To have an opportunity to get in touch with what is going on in the world and to be ready to be employed is much needed in the system. The state senators are the ones that fund the reentry programs that are in the prisons. This is something I can help Diane with. I am very grateful that she asked me to speak. I believe it is part of the ripple effect. Do right, and that ripple will just keep on going.

13

Rippling Reflections

Every week, I call my grandchildren, and they fill up my tank. By this, I mean they fill my heart up with joy. I get Piper, Emily, Anthony, and my little fighter Maddie on the phone, and they make me laugh. I say to them that I love them, and they say, "I love you, Papa."

I ask them, "How much?"

They tell me, "To the moon and infinity beyond."

I love hearing that from those innocent babes. I was talking to Piper one night, and she just wouldn't get her mother on the phone, and I needed to talk to Ani. I said, "Piper, get your mom and put her on the phone."

She said to me, "Okay, Papa, here she is."

Then all I hear is "Hello, this is Ani. Can I help you?" I knew this was Piper imitating her mother, and I laughed my butt off. This went on a few more times before she gave the phone to her mother. I told Piper that she made me laugh, and she told me she liked to make her papa laugh. This is priceless and warms my heart. Right out of the mouths of babes. Piper is only five years old, and I am like, where does she get all the humor from?

To have conversations with these little ones that are between the ages of five to twelve is good for the soul. I tell them that I am in the big house, and they know I am in prison. They have all visited me from time to time, and I am blessed to have such beautiful grandchildren in my life. I have three more grandsons—Miguel, Javier, and Joseph Jr. I can't wait to take them fishing and teach my eldest grandson, Miguel, how to drive.

That ripple effect just keeps on going, doesn't it? Who would have thought that the decisions I had made thirty years ago would have rippled down to my grandchildren living without their grandfather in their lives? Just as my children grew up without me there, my grandchildren only know me as their parents did, by phone calls and occasional visits.

The ripple effect is something that I wish everyone would ponder before making a life-changing decision. Many people do not think about the consequences that their decisions could bring. *Consequences last a lifetime. They just keep rippling down as the years pass by.* Think of the stone that you tossed in the pond. Then you stood there watching as the ripples kept rolling out until you could no longer see them. Life is the same way, my friend. We all toss stones in the pond of life.

My life has not been a waste. It has been a journey. I think that my life has been a crazy trip, but I look forward to seeing what the next chapter has in store. I never again have to slap myself and say, "Man up." *I have become the man that for most of my life I did not have the courage to be.*

Epilogue

As I sit here a free man, I am thrilled to share with you that I made it to work release in 2018. I received a two-year hearing from the parole board. I had a hard time finding a job because no one wanted to give a man who served over thirty-three years in prison a chance. Finally, I landed a good job as a sprinkler installer. I advanced to work as a manager at the owner's estate.

I saved enough to buy that Harley I dreamed about and an old pickup truck. I am in a relationship and engaged. One thing I am proud of is that I enrolled in college to obtain my degree in chemical dependency counseling.

There were a lot of ups and downs over the past few years. I kept the end in mind and never gave up or turned back to the choices that led me to prison to begin with.

The ripple effect continues, and I am excited to start on my next book called *The Ripple Continue*.

About the Author

Thomas Lee Fleming is now paroled and working full-time as a farm manager for his boss's private estate. He is engaged and enjoying building relationships with his grandchildren and family. He just enrolled in college to obtain his chemical dependency counseling degree. He continues to speak at treatment centers and criminal justice classes, sharing his story. He enjoys riding his Harley Davidson and calls it wind therapy. He still struggles with being in large crowds and being surrounded by a lot of people, such as a Walmart. He loves sharing the lessons he has learned and does this in hopes that he can instill the lesson of choices and consequences into one person and help them from entering the dark prison system.